AT THE CROSSROADS
Finding God at the Point of Greatest Need

CHARLES E. CRAVEY

IN HIS STEPS PUBLISHING

Statesboro, Georgia

Copyright © 2024 Charles E. Cravey

All rights reserved. No part of this book may be used or reproduced by any means, graphic, electronic, or mechanical, including photocopying, recording, taping or by any information storage retrieval system without the written permission of the publisher except in the case of brief quotations embodied in critical articles and reviews.

IN HIS STEPS PUBLISHING and Charles E. Cravey books may be ordered through booksellers such as Amazon.com, Booksamillion.com or BarnesandNoble.com.

Because of the dynamic nature of the internet, any web addresses or links contained in this book may have changed since publication and may no longer be valid. The views expressed in this work are solely those of the author and do not necessarily reflect the views of the publisher, and the publisher hereby disclaims any responsibility for them.

Certain stock imagery © istockphoto.com

All scripture quotations are taken from the King James Version of the Bible

Library of Congress Control Number: 2024902247

ISBN: 1-58535-278-0 (ePub)
ISBN: 1-58535-279-9 (Kindle)
ISBN: 1-58535-280 -2 (Soft)

In His Steps Revision date: 03/01/2024

Epigraph

Sooner or later, we will arrive at a crossroads in life, a meeting place where our greatest needs meet with either a simple whisper or an earth-shattering decision. A hospital stay, a doctor's pronouncement, a career change, a mental break, an accident along life's pathway —all these and more bring us to the point where our inner spirit cries out to the creator for a ray of hope and grace.

Charles E. Cravey
March 2024

Dedication

~

*I dedicate this work to all of my readers,
faithful church members, loyal friends, and family.
You are the greatest!*

Contents

Epigraph	v
Dedication	v
INTRODUCTION	xi
Preface	xiii
1. SHORT STORIES	1
The Unyielding Survivor	3
The Busted-Knuckle Garage	5
"Me-Ma's Diner"	9
Reflections on Freedom	13
Testimonial	15
Observations Made at Walmart	21
A Sense of Balance	27
The Darkest Night	31
Tragedy: The Blind Sister of Hope	33
2. POEMS, PRAYERS, AND PROMISES	37
Crossroads of Life	39
"Be Still and Know"	41
The Place You Would Have Me Be	43
In Memoriam	45
Sacred Relics	47
Poetic Justice	49
Code Blue!	51
Lament on Richard Cory*	53

The Bar	55
Handiwork	57
At the Intersection	59
Adjusting the Lens	61
Calm Assurance	63
Pages of Our Lives	65
Over Life's Tempestuous Seas	67
When My Mother Used to Pray	69
Just Reward	71
Peace, Be Still!	73
On the Meaning of Life	75
Harp-Strings of the Heart	79
In This Together	83
Sixty, More or Less	85
All about Grace!	87
The Center Holds	89
Small Packages	91
Paradoxical	93
Awake!	95
Somewhere Ahead	97
In Morning's Solitude	99
Poetry Prayers	101
Yesterday's Passageway	107
Closer than Ever	113
Grace	115
Healer of Our Hearts	117

3. FAITH & PHILOSOPHY — 119
   Love Kindness — 121
   "Shall We Sit Here Until We Die?" — 123
   Life's Little Extras — 127
   That Sense of "Lostness" — 129
   Kathy's Letter — 131
   My COVID Dilemma — 133
   The Capacity to Care — 135
   Call Waiting — 139
   Going Where the Fish Are — 143
   Soft Landings and Smooth Flights — 147
   Right Where You Left Him — 151
   Horse Creek and Other Near Calamities — 153
   Assurances of the Christian Faith — 157
   Fruits of the Spirit — 163
   A Spiritual Fork in the Road — 165

4. BIBLE TALKS FOR DAILY WALKS — 167
   Filled With New Wine — 169
   Giving Alms — 171
   A Thicker-Thinner — 173
   Length of Days and a Long Life — 175
   Bare Necessities — 177
   Rejoice in the Lord Always! — 179
   Take Up Your Cross — 181
   To Lose Your Child — 183
   The Calling — 185
   Be Charitable — 187

The Wages of Sin	189
How to Gain Your Life	191
"Whom Shall I Send?"	193
Trust in the Lord	195
Rejoice, Pray, and Give Thanks	197
Living the Cleansed Life	201
What Can You Offer the Lord?	203
Creating Something from Nothing	205
Just One Rose Will Do	207
The Potter and the Clay	209
Saddest Truth in Scripture	211
A Cure for What Ails You	213
A Monopoly on the Spirit	215
A Clear Conscience	217
Consider the Lilies	219
Speak Truth	221
Endurance in the Wilderness	225
Epitaph	229
ABOUT THE AUTHOR	231
OTHER PUBLICATIONS BY THE AUTHOR	233

INTRODUCTION

There are countless souls facing the crossroads of life today. You may be one of them in search of answers for the confusing world in which we live. We turn to many different sources: the Bible, friends, family, and others, looking for a ray of hope in the midst of our darkness.

AT THE CROSSROADS will explore many souls who have been there before and had to make the tough decisions they faced. Their testimonies and witnesses give us an inner peace and consolation for the journey ahead. There are daily Bible studies that point us in the right direction, articles of faithfulness, and short-stories that move us emotionally as we read of those who have suffered and endured.

There are devotionals contained herein to give insight on our road of life, and how many different people have dealt with making some of their toughest decisions ever.

May you find hope and inner peace within these pages, written by an author who has been there before and shares his experiences with the reader.

God bless you in your journey today.

PREFACE

Sometimes you get lucky and become part of something larger than yourself.

- Billy Dee Williams (of "Star Wars" fame)

I am back again, seventy-two years of age, writing my eighteenth book. I began this journey early in my teens, when I fell in love with the written word. I would later find myself devouring every word like they were bites from a delicious New York cheesecake! Movies and I became a love affair. Dialogues between actors were observed and replayed over and over again in my mind. I would watch every commercial, learning the jingles and words to each. This romance has carried me through these years with grace. I can't stop writing.

Billy Dee Williams, in the quote above, realized at some point he was part of a larger scheme of things beyond his control. Each time I pick up my pen, I realize there is something far greater than myself—magic, if you will—taking place on the page. It is truly a romance that I cannot ignore. It is a paradox between emptiness and fullness. When I set the pen to paper, I am emptied. When I sit back and review the magic, I am filled with awe and amazement at what I have created. And yet, it is not my creation but a coordination of movies, daily newspapers, TV commercials, my college and seminary training, and life, as it has enveloped me for these seventy-two years.

I hope that you will fall in love with life and the written word as much as I have. I pray that something within these pages will touch your heart and instill new warmth within. Take this journey with me, from the very first typed letter to the last. Know that I am thinking about you and your reactions as you read this. I pray for better days for you and a blessed journey.

Dr. Charles E. Cravey, March 2024
Statesboro, Georgia

Chapter 1
SHORT STORIES

"Often when you think you're at the end of something, you're at the beginning of something else."

- the late Fred Rogers

The Unyielding Survivor

During one of my trips to the beautiful and sublime mountains of North Georgia, I made a hike up Black Mountain, just off Highway 60 between Dahlonega and Suches. It is one of my favorite mountains, and I've camped there many times over the years. On this particular occasion, I found a large cluster of boulders on the side of the mountain and noticed something amazing. There, in front of me, stood a huge hickory tree. It was coming out of one of those large boulders and had tentacles spreading out around the boulder. A tree that pushes its way up through a boulder is a remarkable sight. First, a seed falls atop the boulder and finds nourishment in the sandy soil, which has been blown in by wind and rain for years upon the rock. The seed begins its miraculous journey of sprouting and growing, baby step by baby step, until it receives the energy to push even further, often penetrating the cracks and crevices of the rock. Over the years, the small seed becomes a large tree, standing tall against the mountainside.

This process is a testament to the resilience of nature and its will to survive. It is, in essence, the tree's struggle and its eventual triumph over the seemingly insurmountable obstacle of the boulder.

In a similar fashion, the tree's perseverance and determination are qualities that we can all aspire to in our lives. At birth, we were not given instructions on how we should live or grow. We were completely in the care of parents who fed us, clothed us, and gave us nurture. We would not have survived without their care.

I once met a man who had no legs. He had lost both of them in World War II. Upon returning home, after many months of surgeries in a veteran's hospital, he began the long and arduous process of recovery. I was always impressed by his strength and resilience. He was determined to walk again at all costs. He would not allow himself to become cynical or complacent and spend the rest of his life in a wheelchair. He would push himself in rehab to do the daily exercises to strengthen his physical body. Mentally, he was as strong as an ox!

After being finally fitted with two prosthetic legs, my friend began the journey of learning to walk all over again. He pushed himself constantly when others may have given up. His determination finally paid off. He is walking today, and his testament is shared with others who are still struggling to make sense of their own situations.

Sometimes a seed of faith is all it takes—an unyielding survivor determined to grow where planted.

The Busted-Knuckle Garage

(a short story)

Bobby Carter's "Busted-Knuckle Garage" closed for good yesterday. Due to his age and health, Bobby felt it was necessary to give it up after fifty-six years. His faithful and dedicated service had been commendable to the local townsfolk who had trusted him with their cars, trucks, and even an occasional tractor. Bobby was a whiz with mechanical work and would be sorely missed by everyone. He had taken care of Mr. Salter's old '66 Continental since it was first purchased, and Salter had never trusted another mechanic. Bobby knew his vehicles intimately and would miss the work and, yes, the busted knuckles that went along with it!

The closing went without much fanfare. Bobby simply closed the old, dilapidated building and turned the key in the lock for the final time. A strip-mall firm had paid Bobby a premium for the property. The building was scheduled for demolition next week. Soon, nothing would remain to remind locals that it ever existed. The garage would only remain in the minds of the many who had done business with Bobby through the years.

I went by to see Bobby last week, knowing he was closing, and had him service my old '76 Subaru for the last time.

"You need to trade this old tin tub, Darrell, for one of those newfangled e-lech-tronic cars," Bobby told me. "It seems like the entire world is going 'Lectric," he continued. I only had 211,000 miles on the Subaru, and its longevity is owed to Bobby and his expert service! "You are beginning to lose a little oil between changes," Bobby said, "and I feel certain that she's going to need the heads worked on before much longer."

"Who do you suggest as your replacement, Bobby?" I asked. "You're the only mechanic I've ever known and used since my very first car as a teenager."

"Well, there's Phil Clark over in Silver Hill," Bobby replied. "He's a really good mechanic, and I trained him right here at the shop about twenty years ago. I trust him, and he is only fifteen miles from here. Tell him I sent you," he continued.

"We're all going to miss you, Bobby, but I know you're tired and ready to go places with Helen and do some things other than garage work," I said. "Thank you, Bobby, for all you've done for me."

"You'll be okay," he said. "Just stay healthy and be well. You know my health is one reason I am closing the shop, Darrell. I just can't crawl under the cars anymore."

When Bobby turned the key for the last time and got into his '55 Chevy, he headed home to Helen and their Boykin Spaniel, Chip. Driving down East Main, Bobby began feeling a lump develop in his throat. He would sorely miss the old place, for it had been his home for these fifty-six years. Bobby had never become rich running the shop, but he fared better than most in this line of work. He had put money aside each month into his retirement account at Helen's insistence, and it had grown exponentially through the years. He and Helen were set for retirement, and Helen already had plans scheduled for the months ahead.

Where would they start? He wondered. All these years, Bobby had awakened at six a.m. and made his fresh pot of Maxwell House. He would then watch the early news, shower, and make his way to that dusty old shop that smelled like a million oil changes. To Bobby, it smelled like heaven and money! He enjoyed entering the shop each morning and greeting his first customer of the day. He wondered how he would fare without all of that. Would he be content with the Grand Canyon, Yosemite, and the Redwood Forest? Helen had always wanted to go on a cruise to Alaska and see the whales.

And then there were the kids. Little Bobby, as they affectionately called him, was a mechanical engineer in Atlanta with two children, Allison and Ethel. It had been two years since they had made that drive from Franklin to Atlanta, but Bobby knew that Helen was ready to do more of that.

And then there is Grace, who is an interior designer for a high-end design firm in Chicago. She had never married because her life was married to her work. I guess Bobby and Helen would make that first ever road trip to Chicago and stay with Grace for a while. Bobby wasn't looking forward to that trip at all!

Then, there were all the "honey-do" projects at home that Helen had asked Bobby a million times to do for her. I guess he would take them one at a time until he got them done. He figured he would be busier than he ever had been at the garage! A new leaf was being turned in his life, and Bobby was uncertain as to whether he was prepared for it. He knew, however, that his health was such that he had to do something else.

Bobby rode down to "The Busted-Knuckle" two weeks later and sat in his Chevy while he watched the bulldozers push down his beloved Nell, the name he had affectionately given the garage years ago. His heart sank like a ton of bricks as he watched Nell crumble into a heap of rubbish. He still remembered the first day he started his business. Robby Morris from First State Bank in Franklin had given Bobby the key to the building and said, "It is all yours now, Bobby. Take loving care of her." Nell used to be Robby's father's service station until he succumbed to a massive heart attack. Bobby had briefly worked for Robby until his passing.

It was bittersweet watching it all come down today. Things would never look the same around here again, Bobby thought. Soon, the new strip mall would fill this space with shops and busy shoppers, and the future would soon overtake the past.

Bobby sat with tears in his eyes as he watched each dump truck being loaded and then would take Nell away to some landfill outside of town. To Bobby, this had been a sacred place. It was home, and all he knew. His children had written their names on the old whitewashed walls of the building and had drawn little picture of smiley faces and such. It was very difficult for Bobby to see all of that crumble before his eyes. A sad day indeed!

"I can't fuss about the past," Bobby thought. "I got to let it go and get on with my new life." Bobby paused and then said, "Goodbye, Nell." Bobby then cranked up his old car, pulled out onto the highway, and headed home. He kept glancing into the rear-view mirror until he reached his turn at Bellflower Street. It was then that he noticed the little sign printed on the outside mirror, which read, "Objects are closer than they appear." Bobby's life had just disappeared in his rear-view mirror!

"Me-Ma's Diner"
(A Short Story)

Legends are born and die in small towns across America. There are legends, however, that seem to live on forever in the minds and hearts of locals. Me-Ma (aka, Gloria Satterfield) had become such a legend in the small county seat town of Ranger, a town of about 2,000 souls. Folks came 20 to 30 miles away to eat at Me-Ma's because her food was that good. Nothing out of the ordinary, mind you, but it was just the TLC she put into every dish that brought folks in.

Around her tables, decisions were made by politicians, law enforcement officers, judges, and a host of local farmers and townspeople. Gloria had entertained two U.S. presidents, four state governors, state prosecutors, and several secretaries of state. She had served Little League and high school teams, cheerleaders, and had hosted numerous school events through the years.

Gloria's tables were all circular, and her dishes were served on Lazy-Susan's at each table. Her staples were butter beans, squash, boiled okra, field peas, rutabagas, fresh homemade buttermilk biscuits, cheese grits, turnips, collard greens, and corn. These were usually accompanied by the main entrees of country-fried catfish in Me-Ma's special batter (still a secret to this day!). Her crispy fried chicken was always a staple, and folks had been trying to copy her special herbs and spices for years. She would also serve country-fried pork steak over a bed of rice and gravy, in addition to her sauteed Vidalia Sweet Onions.

And there was always Me-Ma's sweet southern tea, served in Mason jars. No one could make it like her! Her food was always mouthwatering and to die for! Southern hospitality and cuisine could always be expected when eating there.

Me-Ma's best seller was those sweet mini pecan pies. Folks would stop by to purchase a dozen or so, even when they did not have time to eat a meal. The pies had become a calling card for Gloria. She had seven pecan trees in her backyard and labored every December to pick up the nuts when the Stuart's were ready. She cracked each of the nuts by hand and put them in bags for storage in her freezer until she needed them at the restaurant.

Gloria had handpicked her kitchen staff for decades. Sally Mae Johnson, however, had been with her from the time Gloria opened the diner. They had both been through a lot of ups and downs through the years, but Gloria had never trusted anyone other than Sally Mae. She and Sally Mae had been best friends throughout school and had graduated together from Carson County High. Three weeks later, Gloria's father had purchased Me-Ma's and helped set her and Sally Mae up with the business. It was an old building at the corner of Main and Hobson Streets. The two worked tirelessly for a month until the opening. Folks had flocked there to eat since the very first day. The diner's fame had quickly grown, and now, fifty years later, Me-Ma's has become an icon in Ranger and parts beyond. People trusted Gloria and Sally Mae because they were always consistent in whatever they served, not to mention how good it was!

Sundays were always the busiest because folks would come into town to worship at either the Baptist or Methodist churches and would be hungry and ready to eat when the services were over. Folks would often tell their pastor to preach "short sermons" so they could beat the other church to Me-Ma's and get a good seat. You knew that something was wrong whenever Me-Ma's food took precedence over a worship service! You see, to many folks, Me-Ma's *was* a worship service! The mere thought of her crispy fried chicken could often rattle even the preacher's best-prepared sermon!

Speaking of church, other than weddings or funerals, Gloria had not attended a church worship service since her teen years. Her religion was the diner, and serving the folks of her community seemed like a fitting way for her to express her beliefs. She never showed favoritism and always spoke to each customer before they left. Gloria would make sure that each child in the diner would receive one of her popular chocolate-chip cookies before they left.

Gloria never married but came close about twenty years ago when Jacob Cross, a widower and local farmer, started courting Gloria each day at the diner. After about a year, Jacob suggested that she give up the diner, marry him, and move to his farm. Well, that was the end of that relationship! Gloria subtly let Jacob know that she was married to her work and that no man could ever take her away from what she loved and lived for.

In fifty years, the only time Gloria had missed work was for jury duty and a terrible bout with pancreatitis. Sally Mae had carried on each time without a hitch. The diner was like a smooth-oiled machine, and folks could always count on it being open whenever they needed a good, hot-cooked meal.

The name "Me-Ma" came from Gloria's affectionate name she called her late grandmother. She had taught Gloria how to prepare and cook southern cuisine to near perfection. Gloria, in fact, began cooking the family meals early in her teens. Her dishes were always a hit with the Satterfield family. Gloria remembered those long Sunday afternoons at Me-Ma's house and her advice about "a little bit of this and a dash of that." She would watch Me-Ma like a hawk and devoured every single recipe. She also remembered Me-Ma telling her that she had to put a little love into every dish. Locals had learned years ago what her secret ingredient was through Gloria's special smile and the love she gave through each plate she served. Your KFC's and Popeye's can sell you a chicken plate, but Me-Ma's serves you a plate with love! Therein was the biggest difference.

Strange winds began to blow in early 2020. Several Washington State nursing home patients had died from a strange and mysterious virus that began spreading across the U. S. like wildfire. Hundreds of people were dying from the virus daily, and most people around Ranger took the warnings from the CDC to wear masks in public seriously. People became alarmed about the virus because it not only affected nursing home patients but otherwise healthy children and adults. There was no end in sight, and there was no antidote to cure it.

Me-Ma's and other restaurants began suffering from a lack of people to serve for fear of catching what would later be called the COVID-19 virus. Some said it came from diseased bats in China, while others heard that it had been developed in Chinese labs to be used in chemical warfare. No one knew for sure, but everyone knew that the virus would kill you.

Days, weeks, and even months went by, with people dying daily from the virus. It had also impacted Ranger, with four deaths already. Gloria had kept the diner open for as long as she could, but eventually had to close the dine-in section. She only offered drive-thru plates for carry-out.

The world was quickly changing for a small town like Ranger, and businesses everywhere were hurting. Some even closed that had been open for many years, and some would not reopen again at all.

Lenny Johnson at the County Clerk's office got the word the other day through the grapevine that Gloria Satterfield had contracted the virus and had been carried to the hospital over in Hampstead. She was now in isolation and could not receive visitors. Within days, a great icon in Ranger had died. Everyone wanted to do something for Gloria and her family, but the virus held them back. A cremation of her body would take place, and a private graveside burial of her cremains would occur in a few weeks. No body, no visitation, no service. Gloria Satterfield and Me-Ma's would soon be a distant memory to the folks in and around Ranger.

Last week, some townsfolk hung ribbons and bows in each window at Me-Ma's, and they hung a wreath on the double doors out front. An entire town mourned her passing.

While Gloria may not have been that religious, Me-Ma's was a religion to the many who would miss the warm smile and dedicated service she always offered. In the annals of history, her name will not be found. But in the hearts and minds of townsfolk, Me-Ma's will always hold a special and sacred place. Rest well, dear Gloria.

Reflections on Freedom
(A Treatise on Immigration)

The late evening sun filtered through the woods in Terra-cotta hues, bouncing from cloud to cloud, revealing gold-tinted skies. Restless spirits stand on the precipice and gaze beyond, looking for deeper meaning, as each cloud moves with uncertainty across the wide expanse. Caught in the moment, I witness this spectacular event in reverent awe, seeking confirmation, while knowing clouds do not speak, colors cannot change a mood, and the sun can only glow and offer its warmth.

Below, I can see the many leaves of fall: sweet gum, maple, red oak, persimmon, sassafras, and poplar. The leaves are like a metaphor for America. This nation is comprised of various races, which make up the cauldron of humanity. We all belong here, and each deserves a place in the sun. We truly reflect the saying engraved on the pedestal of the Statue of Liberty in New York Harbor:

"Give me your tired, your poor, your huddled masses yearning to breathe free." ("The Story Behind the Poem on the Statue of Liberty")

We are pilgrims here upon the precipice, yearning to express ourselves and become a vital part of the whole. We should not be self-righteous and pious, but immigrants, thankful to be part of a free society and to have the excellent opportunity of making something with our lives. We came from dictatorships, communist systems of government, and broken societies. We are the dreamers, following our dreams and seeking the fleeting ideal of freedom. We do not seek to change America, but to make her better.

From rat-infested villages, we come. From countries where starvation is rampant, we come. From abject poverty, we come. We, the "huddled masses," come with open hearts and minds to find "America, the Beautiful." We will become your doctors, research scientists, college professors, and a plethora of other professions, aimed at helping to continue making America greater and greater for generations to come.

You, who have plenty, by whatever means, do not look down upon our dirty, bedraggled children, for you may be looking up into their faces one day from a hospital bed and thanking them for being your doctor! Do not belittle us for digging your ditches, doing your dirty work for minimum wage or less, and harvesting your crops in the sweltering summer sun. Think of us when you are eating that next sumptuous meal and offer a word of thanks. We were not born with silver spoons, but only with the shirts on our backs. We only ask for a chance to be free. We will work from sun-up until sun-down to give our children a chance of a better life.

We are often forgotten or ignored, but we are there in your squalor houses that are falling apart at the edge of some farmer's field. Our children are often ignored in the classroom because they do not speak your language, and the teachers do not speak our language. Give them time, and they will learn.

Politicians use us to help build their cases against immigration. We are all immigrants. Just think of how the early Indians must have looked at your ancestors when they first invaded these shores! They killed so many of them to carve out a new existence. They rounded them up and imprisoned the Indians on reservations that were most inhospitable. Your pilgrims came preaching and teaching an English religion of love and acceptance while pushing the Native Americans further away from your god. How can we believe in such a cruel god as the one you proclaim? The pilgrims burned many of their own people at the stakes, as well as the Indians, because they did not believe in their god. And you say that your ancestors came to these shores to escape "religious persecution?" Please, we are persecuted every single day!

This nation was built upon many injustices. Our "huddled masses" were singled out, separated from their families, put in holding cells under atrocious living conditions, beaten, and many sold into slavery, which would take them over 100 years to gain freedom from.

We are not the "Land of the Free" as long as one single immigrant child remains imprisoned for a crime they did not commit, as long as we continue to ignore their existence among us as fellow human beings, as long as we fail to treat everyone fairly and give them the same opportunities our forebears were given, as long as we continue to ramp up the rhetoric to make those in opposition even madder... Until then, we will not be free!

Testimonial

I stared out my bedroom window tonight at that great ball of light in the sky and felt a fantastic sense of awe and excitement. Poets have written for centuries about the moon. Philosophers have debated its purpose and reason for appearing in our galaxy. Lovers have sat under its spell and promised "the moon" to each other. Ships at sea have been guided safely home and kept on course.

As I continued to gaze upon its beauty in a cloudless sky, I began to remember the news I had heard at eighteen: that man had finally set foot upon that great orb. In fact, two men were walking on that great star! The date of July 20, 1969, will always hold a special place in history as the day that Neil A. Armstrong and Edwin E. Aldrin, Jr. walked on the moon.

Can you begin to imagine that man had traveled over 100,000 miles in a spacecraft and had landed that craft on the surface of the moon? And then, if that was not amazing enough, they walked upon it! It was almost unbelievable as I sat and watched it occur on an old black-and-white TV set.

On this night, while staring at the moon's light, I imagined how those earth men must have felt. Can we begin to imagine their feelings and emotions as they stepped down that ladder and began making the first impressions upon the moon's surface? They had traveled beyond our human existence into a new realm. They had been where no man had been before! Their lives would never be the same again.

While my wife and children slept peacefully in their beds, I stood in the darkness of our bedroom looking at the full moon in all its glory and began to remember such a dramatic and life-changing event in my own life some years ago. In fact, it was the same year that those two astronauts made their journey with one other astronaut onboard with them.

That night is firmly ingrained in my psyche. It was the night that something extremely dramatic, mystical, and earth-shattering happened to me. An eighteen-year-old boy entered a new relationship, and in a matter of moments, he became a man—a new creature.

The tenth grade was a time of great challenge for me. The year before, I had tasted the freedom of being out of school and in the workforce. I enjoyed the work I was doing (beekeeping). It was very intriguing to me. Two of my fellow workers kept encouraging me that year to return to school and make something out of my life. They did not want to see me beekeeping for the rest of my life.

Neither of my co-workers had made it past the seventh grade in school. They had always struggled and wrestled with life to achieve even the smallest of goals.

My friends reminded me of my own family and the struggles we had been through. They wondered how I could be content to remain where I was and remain a mediocre person without accepting the many challenges of life that had been set before me.

I would argue with them that school, for me, was terrible. The teachers seemed unconcerned, and the education was useless. Plainly, my friends let me know that the world was not out to get me, that you get out of life exactly what you put into it; and that if a person tried hard enough, he could make dreams come true. Somehow, I had heard all of that before, but they had never made quite as much of an impact as they seemed to make then.

Who would have thought that it was humanly possible, those many years ago, that man could have traveled to the moon and back and even walked on it? And, too, how could anyone ever make something out of this old "Cravey" boy from Pot-Liquor Hill? Yet, two old school dropouts believed in me enough and felt that I could be someone and accomplish something good in my life. It means a world of difference when another person believes in you and will encourage you to better yourself in life. I had two of them: Ronnie Geter and Mr. William Routh.

Daily, these two men gave their words of encouragement. At the end of that summer, I returned to school and gave it another try with my new-found insight from them.

I entered school that year and felt ill at ease with myself around teachers and students. They were looking down at me for having dropped out for that year, and now I was humbling myself by returning. I threw myself into my studies and began reading more books. I really began to give school more of my time to help me ignore those around me.

A few of my old friends, most of them now in the eleventh grade, spent some time with me and gave me some encouragement. I still struggled within but continued to remember my two friends in beekeeping out there working in the extreme heat, going from bee-yard to bee-yard to make a pittance of a living. That was all the motivation I needed! I could not and would not disappoint them, so I persevered.

I grew increasingly encouraged by a new teacher, who gave me time to write my poetry and present it to her in class. She really took an interest in my abilities, and I was most appreciative. I also had help from two friends who had recently found salvation through Christ in a Campus Crusade for Christ meeting.

I spent more time with these two friends as I began growing more convicted as they shared scripture and bible stories with me. Then they invited me to one of the home meetings of the Campus Crusade for Christ. I was asked to bring my guitar and play for the group of around twenty high school kids. They were simple songs, such as "Kumbaya," "Down by the Riverside," and other popular Christian songs of the day. I could play them all and felt great at being the center of attention that night. The meeting that night was very moving for me. I began to feel a strange, unknown sensation I had never felt before, and it was good!

At the close of the meeting, I was invited by my two friends to go with them to an old church and pray with them before I took them home in my mother's car.

As we entered the church, we did not turn the lights on. Instead, we made our way down the center isle to the altar, where we kneeled to pray. The altar was curved. One friend found his way to the far end of the altar, and the other friend followed suit to the other end. I was left in the middle, in front of the pulpit. We had locked the large double doors when we entered, so we would not be disturbed. My heart was "strangely warmed" that night. A presence entered my life that night that I had never known before. I gave my heart to Christ that night and received His wonderful

Holy Spirit! My life began to come together for me, and it started taking new shape. I would never again be the same!

That school year, I studied the hardest I ever had and grew in God's rich graces. I read John's gospel over and over again until I nearly memorized it. Romans became my favorite, as I found myself in every scripture recorded by the Apostle Paul. Even school took on a new and glorious meaning. I was now alive!

How can a man go to the moon, walk on it, return home, and ever be the same again? Well, in like manner, how can a person meet the master of all creation and be the same again? I had experienced that night, in a darkened old church, the ultimate experience in life and would never relegate it to just some memory of the past!

I became more disciplined in my studies and my personal life. Everything now has a new meaning and purpose for me. I attended Bible studies, seminars, and worship services in various places and just grew so much in the next two years. It was too great and too fast for me to really believe all that was happening in my life—the school dropout!

And then, God called me to preach! Me, a preacher? I was to share my story and His with the world! What a challenge! What a goal to seek in life! To be a messenger for the King of Kings and the Lord of Lords would be the ultimate journey of my life! And I am still doing it 52 years later!

Each time that I confronted my two old beekeeping friends after that, they would hug me and tell me how proud they were of my conversion. I remember that Mr. William Routh came to hear me preach my first sermon at the Helena United Methodist Church. How could I ever let my two friends down? I would press forward in faith to accomplish God's will in my life.

Some years ago, I was asked by the family to return and preach the eulogy at Mr. Routh's funeral service. I was given that opportunity to share my love for one of the men who had made quite an impact on my life and had encouraged me to stay the course. Never think that you are just a beekeeper, a teacher, or a preacher. You make a difference in the lives you encounter each day.

Strange as it may be, a few years ago, I purchased four bee boxes and started my own hives in our front yard. I made honey for three years, sharing it freely with neighbors around me. I kept them until my wife was stung underneath one eye by one of my little critters and said that something had to go—me or the bees! Guess which had to go at that point?

The Apostle Paul reminds us in II Corinthians 5:17: "Therefore if any man be in Christ, He is a new creature; old things are passed away; behold, all things are become new." (KJV)

I could never be the same after giving my life to Christ, and neither can you, beloved, if you truly give yourselves to Him and have a personal relationship with the Father! Your life will change, and God will lead you in a new direction.

I was married soon after my call into ministry. My wife, Renee, and I have two beautiful children, Angela and Jonathan. I only pray that they have heard enough of my sermons that one day they will make their decisions to come to Christ and live the fulfilled life they were created for. When that day comes, I will rejoice, even if I am in heaven by then!

If you are willing to become a new creature in Christ, God will change you and use you to His glory. Your life will have purpose and meaning.

You know, raising bees is like preaching the gospel of Christ! You raise more bees to send out into the world to raise more bees. You preach to call sinners to salvation so they, in turn, will help lead others to the redeeming grace of almighty God! Mr. Routh knew what he was doing all along! God bless him and others like him who give a word of encouragement to those in need.

Observations Made at Walmart

I took Renee shopping the other day at her favorite grocery store, Walmart. I am not really a fan of the big box store or others like it, but it has become the way of life for many of us. The mom-and-pop corner grocery stores are mostly gone, unable to compete with the large chain stores. The personalization is missed by the store owners who knew you and were part of your daily community life. The mom-and-pop stores helped build America. It was also a gathering place for most everyone in the neighborhood. Today, that is sadly missing.

I sat in our truck near the front entrance and began observing the people coming in and out of Walmart. It amazed me at the characters I witnessed. This article gives you a small sampling of those observations. I have used my own discretion to add life to each character and what I imagined their lives were like.

- She was born in a small village in the southern part of Peru, South America. As she pushed her cart full of groceries to the parking lot, I noticed her being accompanied by her young daughter. The daughter, like her mother, was very rotund and was only twelve years old. They loaded their groceries into the back of a beat-up-looking old '92 Chevy van. It was the cheapest used vehicle on the lot when it was purchased. When it was cranked, I noticed a plume of smoke enveloping the entire van. It was sadly burning oil, and on its last leg! They would have to use it, of course, until it would not run anymore.

The two lived with the lady's husband and three other smaller children in a run-down part of town with drug addicts, prostitutes, and other migrant workers like herself. They had been here for over 10 years. The parents worked during the day doing menial farm work for Harold Sellers, a large farmer in the southern end of the county. The work was hard and laborious, and it seemed never-ending. Mr. Sellers had been known to hire many migrants on his farm and to give them all a chance of making it here in the States. In return, he received the best workers possible at low minimum wages.

The lady had spent everything they had earned that week as she paid for her groceries in cash. I had noticed the daughter nibbling on a Golden Delicious apple as they made their way to the van. To her, it was a great treat, like a Snickers bar and an ice-cold Coca-Cola when I was a child. The daughter had never known about Peru, except for what her parents shared with her. As far as she was concerned, she was an American and proud of it.

I watched as their van pulled away, and I said a little prayer for them. God only knows what it is like to walk a mile in their shoes.

- She was little and bent as she made her way into Walmart. I would guess that she was around 80 years old. She walked alone and lived alone. Her children, a boy and a girl, had married over 50 years ago and both lived with their individual families far away from home. The son was living in Washington, D.C., with four children, and the daughter lived in California with her two. They only made it to see their mother at Thanksgiving or Christmas.

Stella, as I will call her, lived a lonely life in a little two-bedroom home in a sub-division on the west side of town. She had retired fifteen years ago from her work at the local hospital. She was a registered nurse and had worked for many doctors in her long and storied career. Her only friend, Clara Barrick, lived two doors below her. They cooked for each other on Saturdays for lunch and talked about the old days and work. Clara had also been a nurse for Dr. Winston Frayer until his death, and then she secured work at the hospital until her retirement.

Life for Stella was uneventful. Her only trip taken on a weekly basis was to Walmart. There she could see all the newest innovations, or the lack thereof, and catch up on news from folks she knew and saw shopping there. It would take Stella over two hours to buy two bags of groceries! She looked at everything and often complained about the ridiculous prices of today's products.

Her arthritis and rheumatism, combined with the small stroke she had last year, was beginning to take a heavier toll on her. She was stricken with scoliosis as a child, and now the vertebrae in her back are deteriorating. That is why she walked and bent over.

She still drove the 1972 Lincoln Continental her husband had bought and maintained until his death in 1989. Since then, Stella has been alone. The Lincoln now sported an antique tag the county gave to drivers with a car older than twenty years. To Stella, this was a badge of honor to have had a vehicle for so long that was still in great shape.

- He walked with a young twenty-something in his arm as they approached the front doors of Walmart. Both of his arms and neck were completely covered with tattoos! How ridiculous to cover one's body with such "art" for the world to see! Harry, the young, balding man, worked at the local K-Mart but did all his shopping here at Walmart! Go figure! His job was unloading the semi-trucks that came in at all hours of the night shift. His girlfriend had been with him for a couple of years now and clung to him as they walked, as though she owned him! They were buying supplies for a trip to Tybee Island and the beach for the weekend. Sheila, as we will call her, had a dear mother who was not crazy about Harry. She had wished that Sheila could have found a more decent-looking man with a better-paying job. Harry dropped out of school in the tenth grade with no ambition or goals in his life. Sheila worked for a local boutique that sold women's clothing.

- Marilyn Chester walked out of Walmart with a limp and a brace on her left leg. The leg was injured in a traffic accident last Thursday on Main Street. She was the culprit who ran the red light and crossed into the path of Roger Tillman, a prominent lawyer in town. He was already filing the appropriate papers, having charged her with reckless endangerment. Marilyn was very distraught and wondered how she would be able to pay whatever costs the court brought upon her. She was of meager means, living mostly on social security and retirement. There was not a substantial amount in her savings account, so she could only pay by the month for whatever it cost. Her Medicare helped pay for her injuries sustained in the accident. She would need a knee replacement before long, and her two broken ribs gave her a lot of pain, especially when she walked.

Marilyn had little appetite for shopping at Walmart. She purchased only a small amount of food to see her through the coming week: a carton of eggs, a slab of bacon, some BeanieWeenies, Campbell soup, and a loaf of bread. Not the healthiest of foods, but sufficient for Marilyn. She lived alone and did not need much to survive. Her husband, Bill, had died last year and had done everything for Marilyn, even the shopping! His unexpected heart attack left Marilyn, at sixty-two, without her life mate, and it had been tough for her these last few months.

- Lester Simpson was sixteen now and had the freedom to drive his dad's car for the first time. His trip to Walmart was the first of his own. He parked the 2012 Toyota Camry as close to the front as he could and walked around the car twice while checking every door to make sure they were all locked. He was extremely careful with his dad's car and wanted to be as responsible as possible. He was at Walmart to pick up two 12-count packs of Coca-Cola and a bag of Ole Roy dog food for "Critter," their English Spaniel. He whistled as he approached the store, elated that he had been trusted by his father to carry out such a task.

His father had gone with him to the Department of Driver Services to take his driving test just two days ago, and he had passed it with excellence! He was excited but scared and cautious at the same time.

Upon entering the store, Lester grabbed the first buggy he found and moved quickly through the store, picking up the items his father had sent him to get. He was feeling a sense of pride for being able to maneuver through town, park the car at Walmart, pick up the shopping items, and return home in near record time!

He had wished that his mother could have been there to see him, but she had died of lymphoma four years ago in Lester's first year of high school. She had been Lester's voice of reason and was sorely missed.

- *Three Hispanics (immigrants from Central or South America) got out of their car and started walking towards the entrance of Walmart. Their clothes were ragged, and their appearance was rough-looking, from their work in the fields today. Two men and a lady walked with a steady gait as they entered the store. In a foreign country, they were looking for refuge, hoping to fit in with this American society and find a place for themselves. Jobs could be found anywhere, for the Americans would not dig ditches, work on farms, or do any of the dirty work they used to do many years ago. These people fill those jobs gladly and will work tirelessly all day without complaint. They are just thankful to be able to work.

As they passed through the doors, I began to wonder about this "new" America. What have we become? Why do we have to rely on immigrants to do our work for us? Where will all this lead in the years to come? The face of America has changed, and so have we.

All these people cross our paths in the crowded ways of life. They make up the potpourri of humanity and the tapestries woven into one America.

A Sense of Balance

At seventy-two, I am finding each day more difficult to maneuver. When I get up from sitting for a while, I wobble and stumble until I can get sound footing. When I am walking, things are just as difficult, and I fear falling. At my age, broken hips can debilitate; broken knees or bones can become devastating. I am learning to be much more careful when I am walking or getting up from a sitting position.

Everything in our universe exists and operates through a sense of balance, doesn't it? Even our cosmos is governed by this sense, or state, and whenever it is manipulated or thrown off balance, we have some form of calamity! Those tiny little mosquitoes that wreak havoc here in the south even function from this sense of balance. Those gigantic planets in space are held in orbit on their axis because of balance. When we are thrown out of balance, then we are in jeopardy, or peril, for the forces around us bombard us without much protection.

Throughout time, as recorded thus far, we have always been quite aware that the laws of balance exist. Sir Isaac Newton stated in his Third Law of Motion that "...to every action there is an equal and opposite reaction." ("Equal & Opposite Reactions: Newton's Third Law of Motion") ("Ballistic Missile Basics - Federation of American Scientists") This truth can be experienced in many ways. Take, for instance, a man who indulges in too much alcohol. As the alcohol begins to take effect, he begins to weave, becomes dizzy, and even has a sick feeling because his body has been thrown off balance because of the substance in his system.

If a passenger train stops on the tracks, suddenly, everything (including passengers) will rush forward! When I am backpacking in the mountains, as I lunge forward up the rugged slopes towards the mountaintop, my backpack is constantly pulling me backwards with the same amount of force that I trudge forward. Everything balances out in nature and in our universe. The law of balance works.

Another truth is that cause and effect (one of the universal laws that govern our existence) was given substance by Ralph Waldo Emerson. *For every cause there is an effect.* To create one molecule of water, you must have two atoms of hydrogen and one atom of oxygen. To have electricity in our homes, the amount of fuel used to produce that electricity is very vital to the overall picture. The account always balances perfectly!

A friend shared with me once that, in nature, there are no profit and loss accounts for everything in nature balances. Although I am not a Charles Darwin fan, his theory of "natural selection" in nature warrants merit. In his theory, Darwin talks about wild creatures and their vulnerability to occasionally losing their sense of balance. If an animal becomes impaired in any way, that animal can expect a quick death. In nature, there is always another creature lurking, waiting to attack and consume. This is not cruelty, but the actual ways of the wild.

At this point, let us also consider some "spiritual" matters in reference to this theory of nature and the universe. You will notice that one cannot talk about heaven without inferring that there is a "hell." If we preach about love, then certainly the opposite element of hate exists. For every person who believes in faith, there is an opposite side to unbelief. One's hope is often balanced by despair. Our courage is balanced by fear.

Finally, think about one's own immortality (the hope of living beyond death and the grave). If we believe in our own immortality, then certainly there is a balance that exists as "mortality."

In the Bible, there is also the implied "law of balance." God's scales of life always balance. If one sows evil, he shall surely reap evil results. If one sins, then surely that person will die for their sins unless they have received forgiveness. If we forgive not our brother or sister who has wronged us, then neither will God forgive us! If we seek to live by the sword, we shall surely die by the sword! Everything is balanced. Even in God's laws.

The purpose of this discourse is for you to see the importance of balance in everything, especially in your personal life. You can learn to master that balance with purposeful living.

I like the illustration of a tight-rope walker. Suppose that a tight-rope walker lost his firm grip on the pole that keeps him balanced on the wire. How long would it take for him to lose balance and topple to his death below? All tight-rope walkers have a custom among themselves that reminds them to "push their fingernails into the pole" while on the wire, knowing that it is their life that hangs in the balance. Never let go of the pole! Never allow yourself to lose balance. The sudden results could be devastating.

From day-to-day, the newspaper reports yet another person who has fallen from the balance beam of life. They have lost their grip on those things that are of vital importance. A young girl decides at fifteen that home is too structured and too rigid for her, so she leaves home for the city, where she hopes to find herself and start a new life. Very shortly thereafter, she finds herself surviving the day-to-day grind of the street by prostituting herself, selling her soul for a loaf of bread and a place to stay, and giving up her innocence— losing the balance beam of home and family!

A young man, angered by his parents, decides to leave home because of his differences of opinion. He drives his car at a high rate of speed down a back highway in anger. A deer crosses the road ahead of him. He swerves to avoid hitting the deer. His car immediately goes into a tailspin. He loses control and crashes head-on into a telephone pole, killing the young man instantly! What a sad note to add as an example of how we lose balance, but one that seems to repeat itself somewhere in this country every day. The newspapers are full of reports from people who have lost their sense of balance and have, as a result, suffered terrible consequences.

It is most important that you and I learn to maintain our sense of balance or pay the price for losing it! Everything is balanced. You must not lose your grip on those things that are most important to you. That can be many different things to different people, but whatever it is, for goodness sakes, do not let go of it! Keep your balance.

THE DARKEST NIGHT
The Epiphany of our Lord (Isaiah 60:1-6)

It was about 2 a.m. on a Tuesday night in 1975 when it happened. I had taken 10 Boy Scouts on a 5-day, 50-mile hike along the Appalachian Trail, and we had camped in our tents for the evening. I was awakened at that time by the loud thunder and visions of lightning striking outside our tent. The soft rain from earlier in the evening was now a thundering roar in my ears, which startled me at first. The campfire had long been out of the rain. Boys in other tents began crying out to me. "Preacher," they called me, "our tent is wet and we're cold!" What was I to do? All my plans suddenly became shattered. How was I to manage 10 scouts in this kind of situation and somehow get them to safety?

I looked at my trail map and saw that a logging road was nearby that would eventually take us to a village about 6 miles from where we were. Our lanterns would not work, and it was pitch-black outside the tent. Somehow God gave me the strength to rustle those ten boys together with their tents and backpacks, and we started down that little logging road with the dirt beneath us washing out around our steps. We were all soaking wet, afraid, and ready to get out of the thunder, heavy rain, and lightning.

I had a small flashlight in my backpack, but the batteries had become wet from the rain and would no longer work. In the dead of night, without any light to guide our path, I somehow managed to find that trail, and we began trudging down it in haste, one foot in front of the other. I thought to myself, The boys will never let me live this one down! I'll never hear the end of it.

About a couple of miles down that little logging road, a faint light appeared in the distance at a home somewhere along the way. Soon the trail turned into a paved road, and I could then clearly see the light brighter and led the boys in that direction. As we passed that house, I could see another light further down that road, and we just kept on going in the driving rain.

We were all exhausted. The rain never slowed down, and neither did the lightning or thunder. After about four more miles, which seemed like an eternity, we saw ahead a very bright light at a street lamp, which signaled the end of the road and the village we sought. An old country store sat there on the corner and was a most welcome sight to behold.

While I banged on the door, the boys leaned up against the log walls of that store and awaited a reply from inside. Soon, an elderly gentleman and his wife appeared at the door with a lamp. Gazing out at us, the older man said, "Boys, are ya'll lost?" I said, "Sir, we've never been more lost in our lives."

I began to tell him what had happened, and he said, "You're not the first group of kids that have been through this same situation and came here to warm up and dry out." I'll open the shed out back for you boys, and you can stay in there and dry out until tomorrow morning. Mrs. Gooch will have a nice warm breakfast for you around 8 o'clock, and we can then get you sorted and on your way again."

What a nice old fella, I thought. There aren't many of them left in our world today, that's for sure!

Mr. Gooch then asked me, "What brought you boys here to my store?" I told him that faint lights here and there down the road led us to him. Mr. Gooch then said, "I put that bright light in ten years ago just so folks could see in the dark and find their way to us. It cost me $10 a month, but it's been well worth it! I'm glad we were able to shine the light again for folks just like you."

That was one of the darkest and gloomiest nights of my life.

Tragedy: The Blind Sister of Hope
(A Short Story)

They were twins, born only 15 minutes apart. Sara was six and a half pounds at birth. She cried out without Dr. Brown having to give her a spank! She was squirming and highly active when the nurse placed her on Carolyn's chest for her to see. She was beautiful in every way! Carolyn had forgotten most of her pain as she looked upon Sara until the next contraction began. The nurse quickly took Sara to the incubator, while the nurses and Dr. Brown dealt with Carolyn. "Looks like the second one is coming!" Dr. Brown said. "I guess it's in a hurry as well."

Carolyn had struggled for the last two months before delivery and Dr. Brown had placed her on complete bed rest. She had been completely miserable during that time and poor James, her husband of four years, had been an absolute angel to her. He had looked after her every need, giving her baths at night, cooking all the meals, and even hiring Nancy Drake to come and sit with her during the day. James was an engineer at a large Atlanta firm, and the work was very demanding. He was torn these last two months with wanting to be with Carolyn as much as possible, while his work also kept him busy. James had not had a break for a long time, and it was beginning to show. He hoped that once they returned home, he could get a little more quality sleep. I guess he had not thought about the rigors of two newly born children, diaper changes, feeding schedules, and the total commitment that one must make with newborn children. He would find out soon enough.

Within minutes, Carolyn would deliver the second child, also a girl. She had already been named Rosalyn, after her Na-Na, Carolyn's mother. At birth, Rosalyn had difficulty breathing, and the nurses had to take one of those instruments that cleared her nostrils. Dr. Brown was genuinely concerned that the child did not have the reflexes Sara had. She also weighed only 3 pounds, six ounces. Without even letting Carolyn see her, the nurses took her immediately to a glass-encased incubator and hooked her up to an IV for fluids. Carolyn was very emotional at this point and asked Dr. Brown, "What's wrong with her, Doc?" Dr. Brown responded, "We just need to monitor her and run some tests before we know anything, Carolyn. It is all precautionary," he said.

Dr. Brown also alerted Carolyn to the child's weight and the concern he had about that. "It is not unusual," he said, "that one of a set of twins might not be as big as the other at birth." Dr. Brown had not seen this situation before in his nine years as a pediatrician and needed a second opinion, so he asked one of his nurses to call in Dr. Bishop. Dr. Bishop was one of the leading pediatricians in Atlanta and would be able to tell Dr. Brown what was wrong with little Rosie.

Dr. Brown delivered the afterbirth, sewed up the episiotomy, patted Carolyn on the shoulder, and told her that he was off to deliver another child next door but would return as soon as that delivery was over.

James Miller had been told the news about Rosalyn by Dr. Brown before he had been allowed back in the recovery room. Not knowing what the score was, he entered the room with a big smile, hugged Carolyn, and gave her a kiss. "Congratulations, honey! Dr. Brown told me that we have two incredibly beautiful girls," James told her.

"Yes," Carolyn replied, "But I am concerned about little Rosie, James. Is she going to be all right?"

"Sure," James said. "We will know more tomorrow morning, but do not worry your little head about something that is out of our control. God will take loving care of her." Carolyn and James Miller were both Christians and regularly active in their local Methodist Church. Carolyn played the piano, and James was the Sunday School Superintendent. They were married there at St. James Methodist, and both were well known and loved in their community and church. Prayers had been offered up to heaven on their behalf, and there were cards and flowers already in their room from church members and friends.

The following morning, Dr. Brown entered the room early to tell James and Carolyn the news. Rosie had just passed and could not be revived! He and Dr. Bishop had worked for two hours or more trying to save her, but she had succumbed to a condition they called Sudden Unexpected Neonatal Death (S.U.E.N.D). He talked about how rare it was and how they had worked feverishly to keep her alive but just simply could not. It was out of their hands. An autopsy could be performed to verify the cause of death but James and Carolyn opted out. They did not want little Rosie's body defiled in that way.

Two days later, Carolyn and James were allowed to take Sara home. Sadness for little Rosie filled their hearts, and the trip home was bittersweet. Instead of adjusting to life with two new infants, now they would be facing a funeral for one of them. An entire community was in grief. What a tragedy!

Pastor Cromwell from St. James Church came by the Miller's house later in the afternoon to pray with the couple and to hopefully offer much-needed consolation for them. How does one give hope amid such grief? It was a daunting task, and Pastor Cromwell had prayed for God's guidance on his way to the Miller's.

Nancy Drake was at the Miller's home when Pastor Cromwell came. She joined James and Carolyn in a circle while they took hands and prayed with the pastor. It was the most heartfelt prayer they had ever heard. Pastor Cromwell quoted Psalms 23 to the couple, who knew it well, and he spoke of the "valley of the shadow of death" and the fact that God had seen little Rosie through that valley, bringing her safely to the other side. It offered a bit of comfort to the couple, but their grief was overwhelming at this point.

It has been said that hope can emerge from our darkness and despair. The Millers would have family members and church members who would love and comfort them in the days to come. Some poor souls have no one.

Tragedy and hope are two sides of one coin. Sara and Rosie lived in their mother's womb for nine months, each given the same sustenance, even having equal opportunities of being born whole and complete. One child is born with hope and a bright future while the other child becomes the recipient of tragedy. Tragedy and hope are opposites from the start.

For us, tragedy and hope make up the human experience. Many would say that without tragedy there could be no hope. They are two halves of the same heart, the light and the dark, the bitter and the sweet.

The two, tragedy and hope, are the storytellers of our souls. They are the poetic cries of the living and the dying. When the roads of life are hard and long, they are the reasons we continue to move forward. In the midst of our faith, they are the reasons we continue to believe, to press forward to that higher calling in life, and to come to terms with life as it trounces around and makes its way through our pain and joy. Life can be harsh and cruel, but we are told that joy comes in the morning. Tragedy and hope: both metaphors of our lives. Judgmental - compassionate. Physical - spiritual. Crucifixion - resurrection. Suffering and pain - happiness and joy. Tragedy is blind but hope becomes the eyes through which we see. There is hope, even in the midst of our suffering.

God bless you on your journey today.

Chapter 2
POEMS, PRAYERS, AND PROMISES

Poetry lifts the veil from the hidden beauty of the world, and makes familiar objects be as if they were not familiar.

Crossroads of Life

Where cross the crowded ways of life,

Saint and sinner meet.

Crossroads beckon one to choose

Which road, which path, which street —

Down which, each one must reckon;

Decisions made—move on.

Commit to fate or fortune.

The future is yours alone!

"Be Still and Know"
(Psalms 46:10)

When your long nights have ended,

And daylight is what you see,

Your prayers have now been answered

And your spirit has been set free;

Just look to the Master Who calms the storms,

And praise Him for His peace.

Because of Him, you are justified.

And your storms have all now ceased.

Seek Him with your whole heart.

With your life, declare His name.

For He is the Lord of the Universe,

And His grace and mercy reign.

Meditate upon His promises,

Delight in His holy Will;

And He shall calm your stormy seas

And those waves shall soon be still.

Be still, my friend, and hear His voice.

Let Him calm your soul today.

Remember His timeless statutes,

That will never go away!

Trust in His words of comfort

And hope with a blessed heart,

And know His grace will overcome.

And from you it shall never part.

The Place You Would Have Me Be

All I know is that I love you.

Unto thee I will give my best;

Give my life and all within me,

For you are my blessed rest.

Many roads are paved with danger.

But you go ahead of me.

I shall walk the straight-and-narrow

To the place you would have me be.

There is wonder and beauty

In the things that this world holds.

But I know that you are with me.

And I will never lose control.

There is a place of sweet surrender –

And it is the place you would have me be!

In Memoriam

The angels up in heaven opened wide the gates for you!

My brother, now your earthly journey here below is through.

The pain and all the suffering that you endured each day,

Has now ceased; there is perfect calm; the storm has rolled away!

You loved this life abundantly and gave it all you could.

Whenever you were called upon, you responded if you could.

You took not life for granted; full of zest, you lived each day.

With a melody within your heart, you sang along life's way.

Your music, church, and family gave you consolation well.

You always gave so willingly, and your testimony tells

Of how you loved our God above and trusted in His grace.

Within your heart, you always knew one day you would see His face.

We are saddened by your leaving, but we know it is for the best.

With all the pain that you endured, now you deserve the rest.

And we will not soon forget the man who was faithful to the end.

The angels came and took him home. He met death as a friend!

We know that in that Angel Band, he has joined today.

There he sits contentedly, and with angels he will play.

So, as we struggle on each day, somehow, we will always hear

That angel chorus gently sings, and we will always know you are near!

Sacred Relics

Battered fortress,

Archaeologists' find;

Desert fragments

Of forgotten times.

Rocks cry out,

A story to tell

Of some forsaken age:

Some human, living hell!

There embedded

In sandstone and clay,

Are bones that cry-out

To be heard today.

And so, my friend,

With each generation

We dig up the past

To find our creation

Some moment in time,

Sealed fate forever;

Now exposed, unearthed,

Those bound ties were severed.

Dig, not in the past

To find your quest.

Be content in the present

And therein, find rest!

Poetic Justice

Inch by inch,

Day by day,

Season in and out:

The tiny seedling pushes ever upward.

Its growth weaves its way

Around rocks and hardened earth,

Ever pressing forward

Taking nurture from the earth.

Finally,

It breaks the surface and

Emerges against the sun.

Still upward its growth,

Surviving near calamities of lawnmower,

Trodden feet pressed near,

Barren sun,

Lack of moisture:

Until finally,

Its blossoms open

Revealing beautiful flowers

That grace my trellis wall,

All but for a moment in time!

It cries to be seen, admired, and loved -

Poetic justice.

CODE BLUE!

Flashing lights and metal carts
Are wheeled into the room;
Signals of a failing heart,
And one's impending doom.

Angels, white, rush to and fro,
Hectic pace to save;
Another victim slowly goes
Beyond the bright light's haze.

My heart is fading extremely fast.
It signals my "Code Blue."
I pray for rescue now, at last.
Could my angel of mercy be you?

O heart of my heart, vital sign,
Take now my being and make it thine!

Lament on Richard Cory*

He had it all together,

This "Richard Cory" man.

With grace, he wooed the crowds that he passed by.

Silken threads from head to toe,

And gold upon his hands;

We stared at him and asked the question, "Why?"

Why should one so lucky

Be singled out by all?

And why, pray tell, does he deserve the best?

We sat him on a pedestal,

And leaned against the wall.

By him, we judged most of the rest!

But was he really lucky

To be born with silver spoons,

Which fed him from the finest tableware?

Or was it a curse

To be blessed so soon,

And to never have earthly cares?

Oh, cursed life of struggle

That we must live each day!

Yet, sanely, we move against the pain,

And pray for better days!

*Adapted from the poem, "Richard Cory"
by Edwin Arlington Robinson,
(1869-1935)*

The Bar

It seemed so distant to me as a child.

I would stand and gaze at it from a schoolyard view

And wonder its purpose.

Always lurking there on the broad horizon.

I had no time to worry or fret its existence.

Childish things then prevailed.

As an inquisitive teen,

I became the guru-philosopher,

Spouting rhetoric and rhyme about its mystique;

Captivated by its mere presence

Growing closer and closer to the shore.

We hailed it as that invisible mark,

As we sat in college hall rows

And we drafted our theses for the world.

And then, my father died!

I stood on the crest, slowly watching him

Disappear from sight -

I grew angry at that all-impending light!

His lifeless, cold, and stiffened body

Lay there motionless, dead!

I did not understand.

Nor do I to this day.

The mystery of that compelling bar

Which one passes beyond

On one's journey to sea and star.

Now I sense the ebb and flow

Of its approaching call,

As I stand before the wrinkled glass,

And view the man I have come to be.

Blindly now, through a dark veil,

I reach for its beckoning hand

And cross the bar!

Handiwork

Skilled craftsman by his trade,
He dealt in earthenware.
Each curve he shaped and made
With the tenderest of care.

Days and hours long he toiled
To make his work complete,
Never ceasing, fearing foil,
The shards lay at his feet.

When finally, he stood in awe,
And gazed upon creation.
He then believed in what he saw:
His finest heart's obsession!

The handiwork of labored souls,
Complete when in thine hand you hold!

At the Intersection

For a moment today

I felt a world of emotion

Flow through my being,

Stimulating old thoughts of

A distant past and you.

Could it have been you at the corner today?

Could you have returned

To give your belated apologies

For leaving?

I cringed within as I neared

The intersection where time and memory

Crossed in syncopated rhythm.

My heart fluttered for that moment

As the present meets the past,

Then you were gone -

Caught-up in the traffic flow of our lives,

Lost in the clamoring crowds of a

The world that draws us ever apart

Separating emotion from meaning.

I caught one final glimpse of the past

As I watched, longingly, down Crescent Avenue,

And saw you turn one last time

And look towards me as

Though a smile graced your face,

I reached-out in despair with

Beckoning hands to the past:

And in traffic-rhythm

I moved on with my life!

Adjusting the Lens

Apertures to increase light,
Focus on the chosen view.
Lens to capture moments bright,
And visions now of you.

Photographs and memories
Is all I have today,
Reminding heart and soul of you,
My love has flown away!

On distant shores, I stand alone,
And gaze through endless scope;
Knowing now that you are gone,
But still, my heart does hope!

Adjust the lens, through darkened veil,
To view the past wherein you dwell!

Calm Assurance

A calm arrives before the storm,

Sensing nature's blows.

One seeks for shelter, safety, and warmth.

A place where one can go...

To find that calm assurance

From the outer fears within;

Strength for one's endurance,

Where faith begins again.

I have found that in your sweet embrace,

A refuge from life's cares.

Your tender love has found a place

Among the wheat and tares!

O, Love that will not let me go,

Assurance from the storms that blow!

Pages of Our Lives

Seasons change, and life goes on.

Children play, and we sing our songs.

Melodies we wrote upon

The pages of our Book of Life.

Go your way and I will go mine.

Pray that we may one day find

A token chance we will meet again.

And then, as friends, we will share

The pages of our lives.

That same old sun that we knew then

It will never be the same again.

But we will always be dear friends,

Until one day, we meet again.

A special time we shared as one,

We made our place under that old sun.

Working hard, yet knowing then,

All good things must one day end!

Go your way and I will go mine.

Pray that we may one day find

A token chance we will meet again.

And then, as friends, we will share

The pages of our lives.

Over Life's Tempestuous Seas

Over life's tempestuous seas, I have come,

And through the darkest night,

Yet, I have never traveled blind,

For Jesus was my sight!

And when the waves would o'er me roll,

His saving hands I knew

Would comfort and calm those raging seas,

And always bring me through!

Whenever life's unending pain

Prevails upon my soul,

I will never fear; my Lord is near,

To keep my spirit whole!

Onward, then, I go my way,

Through all my pain and fear,

Yet, knowing all the live-long day,

My Lord is always near!

Dear pilgrim-soldier of the Cross,

While traveling through this land,

Never once forget our Lord,

And his loving, nail-pierced hands!

For they will never fail you!

He is closer than a friend!

And He will always comfort you,

And keep you until the end!

When My Mother Used to Pray

The roads of life are narrow, they seem to wind forever.

And men have often tried to go alone.

But the dangers and the trials, heartaches and the sorrows,

Are much too hard for us to bear alone.

So, we would often follow some preordained direction.

We are looking for the strength to guide our way.

But for me, my mind goes wandering, back to home and mama,

And the strength I would find when my mother used to pray!

She would pray for better mornings and rain clouds without warning!

She would ask the Lord to help her children all along life's way.

And she would never forget His blessings

And all the times he would help her.

Oh, I remember when my mother used to pray.

I can still see mama sitting there in her old, gray-flanneled gown,

Mending clothes and shelling peas after we had gone to bed.

Her days were long and tiresome, but she never once complained.

She never had much in her life because she gave it to us instead!

Her faith was always strongest when the storms of life would come.

She would hold us close and pray that the storms would go away.

Her faith now dwells within my blood,

And her life runs through my veins.

Yes, I remember when my mother used to pray!

Just Reward

Just reward for job well-done,

You took the trophy in hand;

And gave your soul to the teeming crowd,

To that chattering bandstand.

Off you went upon your way,

Through passages of time,

Content to know that all your life

You would live with one purpose in mind.

That very end to which you came,

An example of all we are:

Hung your love upon a cross,

Your kingdom upon a star.

Your job now done, in evening sun,

Trophy received as planned;

How could you have known your just reward

Would be nails within each hand?

PEACE, BE STILL!

Troubles in the evening, I have had them all day through;

They seem to bear so heavy on my soul.

But I have found a Savior who has promised to be true.

And He will always be my stronghold.

Peace, be still; Peace, be still!

When the storms of life all come my way,

I will stay within His will.

Peace, be still; Peace, be still!

I will trust in my Lord and Savior,

Peace, be still!

There is no use running, my brother, from the trials in your life.

Just bring them all to Jesus, friend, today.

For He never promised a garden that was free from sin and strife.

But with our trials, He would make a way!

On the Meaning of Life

Strive for happiness, friend.

There is little comfort in great riches,

They are as fleeting as time itself.

The ladder of success can never compare

To the richness of friends made,

Love received,

Shared lives.

One finds life through giving

And not in taking.

Be a giver of all the graces given to you,

And truly, you shall be

The richest of all humankind!

The grace supplied to you shall be

Your comfort and strength,

Your lighthouse in the darkest night,

A friend when others have failed you.

Strive for that which is

Far greater than life itself and

You will find the true meaning of peace.

In a humble, contrite, and serving spirit,

You shall find life and the

Deeper meaning of eternity.

Our mortal lives are as but

Grains of sand along the shore

Washing to-and-fro with every wave,

Being deposited,

Uplifted,

Moved again until, finally

Being broken into millions of atoms and

Becoming part

Of the whole of life!

We must continue

Day after day,

Year after year,

Striving for the best in happiness,

In grace,

In love...

For peace,

Hope

And friendship.

Therein

Lies the hope of eternity . . .

And the very face of God!

Harp-Strings of the Heart

Plucked for resonance,

Sound extrudes,

Melodious tunes, in part;

Soft vibrations,

Gentle persuasions,

Harp-strings of the heart.

You pulled and tugged,

Gave hope to

These cold, hard strings of mine;

Brought endless joy,

The Craftsman's ploy,

Sweet melodies in time.

In dark depression,

My own recession,

I had but all given up.

Yet soon I heard

Harp-strings and words

That filled my barren cup!

In contemplation,

Situations

Sought to rule my day;

Endless quests

And little rest

It drove my heart astray.

But softly still,

Against my will,

You plucked your melody.

Convincing darts

Thrown at my heart,

You set this captive free!

With gentle care,

You worked your ware,

And soon, my heart gave way.

Received the gift,

Sweet spirits lift

My soul unto thy way!

Play ever on

Thy rapturous song,

Imploring unto me

That life is for living,

'Tis far better giving

Your life as a symphony!

Each string of the heart,

A most vital part,

Played out in rhythm and rhyme;

Seeking its place,

In humanity,

A prodigal in his own time...

Cries out to be heard,

Through each note and word,

Expressed upon the harp-strings;

Until final rest,

The poem has been blessed.

Both the poet and poem now

SING!

In This Together

The one who scratches your back,
Scratches my back just as well.
The road with good intentions
Is the road that leads to hell.
The spade that digs your resting place,
Perchance should dig mine too.
So, we are all in this together
Underneath a sky of blue.

The bank that hoards your riches,
Takes my money for the bills.
The road that we both travel
Is the road that one day kills.
No matter what you are seeking
Be assured, I seek it too.
And we are all in this together
Underneath a sky of blue.

Your happiness depends upon

My happiness, you see;

Our lives are all related.

Be it bond man or set free.

No matter where you go or

No matter what you do,

You will find that we are all together

Underneath a sky of blue!

Sixty, More or Less

The following song-poem was inspired by a very faithful and loyal member of my church. He had once asked me to consider writing a theme song for our Senior Citizens Group. I did so and performed it for the group a month later. Some months later, my friend left us to be with the Lord.

Some people think that gray hair is a sign of growing old.

But we've got a new philosophy; it makes us wise and bold!

We will not give up; we will stand our ground and work harder day-by-day

To bring God's kingdom here on earth and show a better way!

We are sixty, more or less, for we have stopped counting age!

We are young and old, alive and bold, just going through a stage.

We are children of the Father, and we are still too young to rest.

We are workers for the Kingdom—sixty, more or less!

Do not look at us with sympathy, for we are not through here yet!

And chances are that we will do more than you would ever bet.

Age is not a factor in our simple loyalty.

Our bodies may be aging, but in the Lord, our hearts are free!

All about Grace!

I'm like the dead among the living,
But I put on a happy face.
All my friends are so forgiving.
They say it's all about grace.

But in this deep despair I'm trying
To keep my head above it all!
Sinking deep in dark depression,
I hear His Call, I hear His Call, and it's
All about Grace. It's all about Grace.
It's all about Grace...

Now, I know where I am going . . .
My Father waits just down the road.
With His arms He will come and greet me,
And He will lift my heavy load!

The Center Holds

While America falls apart and fake news fills the air,

It is hard for one to breathe, and harder still to care.

We are crumbling and kneeling to gods who do not exist,

While America takes the sucker punch and lives in dark distress.

We have been sold a pack of lies which cuts deep in the soul,

Our narcissistic leaders each day become more bold.

Their followers are brain-dead—a cult they have become.

Where are the true believers who once preached God's kingdom come?

Well, I am here to tell you that our faith has never died,

Although fake "Christians" have persecuted us and tried.

But we will not lose the "center" where Christ has always been.

We will hold to God's unchanging grace; the "center" always wins!

Small Packages

Enamored by the pool of reflection,

Narcissus gazed so long

Until he died of utter starvation,

He knew not where he belonged.

One who is wrapped in selfish desires,

It makes a small package, indeed.

Will die by the same pool of reflection,

Plagued by such selfish needs.

Gaze not long at your mirror-like finish.

Turn not away from my love.

It cannot be found in inward reflections,

But through grace from our Father above!

Paradoxical

She loves the seashore.

I love the mountains.

She loves the sunset.

I love the sunrise.

There are no living martyrs.

AWAKE!

Awake! My sullen soul, awake!

There is much to do on this day.

The future is just ahead.

And you must rise from comfort's bed for

Life awaits beyond the bend!

Somewhere Ahead

Cart-man pushes life along,

Always singing a pauper's song.

The destination is yet unknown.

There he goes, and then he is gone.

How wittingly we push our lives

Beyond the pain, we each must strive

Uphill, down valley, somewhere ahead

Until we find our sacred bed.

In Morning's Solitude

Dogs barking down wooded lane

Breaking silence, early morn.

Mist begins its early rise as

Earth awakens to the

Sounds of the night's afterglow.

Embers still flicker

In the consciousness of thought,

It evokes memories of yesterday

When we basked in their warmth and glow,

And life was young and impervious —

days ahead, when fate will change.

You left me when the embers died.

In solitude, I sat and cried.

POETRY PRAYERS

(Four-line poetry prayers, each intended to stand alone)

I am so glad salvation is free

To all who will receive!

Seek from the Father His grace divine,

And He will send comfort to thee! AMEN

I would rather walk in the darkness with God

Than to walk alone in the light.

I would rather walk by faith in God,

Than to walk alone by sight! AMEN

O day of rest and gladness,

A blessed day of joy and light.

The day of my salvation,

When Jesus made all things right! AMEN

Today, on weary nations,

God's heavenly manna falls;

To holy convocations,

His silver trumpet calls. AMEN

To Holy Ghost be praises,

To Father and to Son;

The Church, her voice upraises,

To Thee, blessed Three-in-One! AMEN

Often, when my soul is weary,

And the days seem so long.

I just look up to my Pilot,

And I hear His blessed song! AMEN

Though the night is dark around me,

I am safe because he is near.

Never shall my foe confound me,

While hearing the Savior's voice, I heard! AMEN

God's wonderful grace is all complete.

He supplies my every need.

When I sit and learn at the Master's feet,

I am free! Yes, FREE INDEED! AMEN

If you have tried and failed in your efforts,

Hands are sore and scarred from life,

Just take up the cross of Jesus.

He will remove your pain and strife! AMEN

It is all that I must trust Him

Through every stormy way,

Even when my faith may waver,

I will trust in Him each day! AMEN

In amazement, Lord, I stand before

Your throne of life is divine.

Take me, Lord, and use me today

That I may be fully Thine! AMEN

As you stumble through life each day,

You can always be assured that

If, in Christ, your sins have been washed away,

He will help you to endure. AMEN

To higher ground, He leads me on

Each step that I take today.

His grace is sufficient; I shall not want.

I will trust in my Lord every step of the way! AMEN

Ever nearer to Thy Throne,

I seek to be each day.

Lord, help me as I travel on.

Protect me, Lord, I pray. AMEN

Today I look to my Savior.

I am strong when He is by my side.

I will yield myself fully unto Him,

And in His sweet grace abide. AMEN

Friend, lay your burdens down today.

And come boldly before the throne of Christ.

Trust in the Savior's love divine,

He will grant unto you new life! AMEN

While in my days of sorrow,

And in these valleys below,

I simply look up to Jesus.

He leads me and guides me, I know! AMEN

Beyond the woes of this fleeting life,

There is for us a better home;

A lovely place where peace shall reign,

And tears shall never come. AMEN

Come away, my friend, to a better life.

Give Jesus complete control!

He will grant His grace and love divine,

And He will mend your broken soul! AMEN

Jesus is ready, friend, whenever you call.

He is waiting for you today.

Come to the well of eternal life,

Be saved and made whole this day. AMEN

There is a beautiful melody

Within my heart today.

It is a song of Victory,

Jesus has taken my sins away! AMEN

I thank God for His redeeming grace,

And I will always sing His praise.

For some day, I will see His face.

Thank God! I am saved today! AMEN

Out of my darkness, I cry to you.

Heavenly Father, hear my earthly plea.

Fill me with hope and courage today.

And help me to follow in your holy way. AMEN

Lord of the universe, Father of All,

Guide, Lord, our footsteps so we may not fall.

Walk, Lord, beside us each step of the way.

And we will live, Lord, for Thee this day! AMEN

Yesterday's Passageway

Empty.

Destitute.

Broken fragments of what

Once existed.

The gnawing disturbance of

Unadulterated silence

That rips and tears at my

Own mentality and space

Again,

Serves its remembrance

Upon heart and soul

That is what once existed

It is no more!

GONE FOREVER!

Void.

Without substance.

Without any true meaning of life

Beyond mere survival.

I grope at the latch

Upon the weather-boarded door

Which has withstood the eons of time,

And opened a keg of lost memories,

Sights,

Sounds,

Adventures.

I can faintly recall now

My last venture through this passageway

To life beyond its confines.

The feeling of freedom

From this prison of sorts,

All too well

Remind me that the prison was not

In this place,

But within my own mind!

There, the cell existed.

As I clamored through those early years of

Trial and error,

Valley and hill,

Life and death!

The voices now of that distant past

Cry out from these rugged walls

A resounding reverberation of

Woe and forewarning.

It is day,

But, Oh, my soul,

It is yet darkness!

Here in this cell,

I recall and hear those voices

Moan their weary and forlorn

Tales of the past that haunt me still,

Rips and tears at my being

And seeks to destroy

The saneness with which I have known.

As I pass through the entrance,

Across broken boards

Through which I

View the deadened earth below;

Deadened through the ages of

Darkness and lack of life

I pause to catch my breath,

For I nearly faint at the

Overwhelming power

Of this emptiness —

This void in my life!

"Speak!" I cry.

"Tell me of your woes."

The voices remain

Empty!

Lifeless!

Void.

This valley of dry bones

Will not live again!

Within

I find everything

Virtually as I left it.

But one can never go home again!

Gathering dust

Accumulated through the years,

Dull the memories —

It leaves me feeling

VOID and EMPTY!

I turn

And leave now

With feelings of remorse,

As though grieving over a

Loved one;

For that is indeed what has happened.

There,

In that voided emptiness of the past,

I lost a dear part

Of myself.

I had returned

Only to find that it is

GONE FOREVER!

As I close the weather-boarded

Door of the past,

I leave

For the last time

YESTERDAY —

And crawl

Slowly back

Into the cell of Today!

Closer than Ever

When you're down and discouraged, look up to the Savior.
He'll give you peace, joy, and hope from despair.
Open your heart, friend, and yield to the Father.
And His Spirit will keep you in the Savior's sweet care.

Why should we worry when He cares for the sparrow?
He lifts up the fallen and restores us within.
Never give up, for he's closer than ever.
Confess; He'll forgive you for all your sins.

When life seems to crush you, just rest in His goodness.
His mercy abounds for those who obey.
Just look to the Savior, for He'll never leave you.
He'll help you brighten your long, darkest day!

GRACE

Grace is a mystery that meets us where we are.

But it never leaves us where we are found.

It goes before us and hinges on a star.

And it covers the pauper and the crown!

Healer of Our Hearts

We're amazed at how he does it, every day his blessings flow,
Filled with joy and gladness so that everyone will know;
How his Spirit lives within us, and his love will never part.
He's the Alpha and Omega. He's the healer of our hearts.

Healer of our broken spirits, the calm upon our sea;
He's our strength when we are weakest, and His grace has set us free.
He's our constant in the darkness, and he will never depart.
We owe our lives forever to the healer of our hearts!

He was crucified on Calvary to redeem the souls of man.
There he suffered agony to fulfill the Master's plan.
Now his grace dwells within us, we're his masterpiece of art.
He has touched our wounded spirits. He's the healer of our hearts!

So, we'll praise his name forever, and we'll stand and testify
To the one who brought us liberty, in his love we will abide.

Chapter 3
FAITH & PHILOSOPHY

Faith is taking the next step, although you can't see the path ahead. Philosophy searches for the meaning of our journey.

--Dr. Charles E. Cravey

Love Kindness

A portion of scripture in Micah 6:8 says that we are to *"love kindness."* This must be the most basic and minimal requirement of all religions. It should be our bounden duty to treat other people as we would like to be treated.

Stephen Grellet, an old French Quaker missionary, once expressed this call of kindness over two centuries ago when he said:

"I expect to pass through this world, but once; any good thing therefore that I can do, or any kindness that I can show to any fellow creature, let me do it now; let me not defer or neglect it, for I shall not pass this way again." (Stephen Grellet, Oxford Reference)

All good religion must begin at this point of kindness. We will certainly never agree on everything, and indeed, we may have some areas of our lives in which we are in sharp conflict. We can at least treat each other with civility and simple human kindness. The Bible places no absolute limits on our kindness. God's Law requires that we also extend kindness to one's enemies. In the Old Testament, we see that Exodus 23:5 requires helping an enemy get his donkey back to its feet. Exodus 22:22 requires the children of Israel not to oppress strangers, with the reminder that they were once strangers as well. In Matthew 5:44, Jesus said, "Love your enemies and pray for those who persecute you." (KJV) Therefore, we are not to place limitations on the kindness we show or give. We are to even pour out acts of love and generosity toward those whom we may deem undeserving. For Christians, this is particularly significant because we believe that God poured out His love on us when we were yet undeserving (Romans 5:8).

Kindness is among the most basic requirements for a believer. Even when it is met with cold ingratitude from the recipient, we are still willing to extend it. As someone once asked, if you were given a dollar for every kind word or deed that you said or did and then had to give back fifty cents for every unkind word or deed, would you be rich or poor? We are called to love kindness.

Show some kindness along your path of life today to others, and you will receive the kindness of God in return. Be loyal, faithful, and loving Christians, and God will bless you.

As the late singer Glen Campbell used to sing, "You've got to try a little kindness; yes, show a little kindness. Just shine your light for everyone to see." He realized the immense importance of everyone showing kindness and letting others see the kindness in us. Be the light!

"Shall We Sit Here Until We Die?"

One of my favorite Old Testament scriptures is found in Psalm 46:10:

"Be still and know that I am God: I will be exalted among the heathen, I will be exalted in the earth. "(KJV)

I often remember the passage when life becomes rushed and overly hectic. I remind myself to stop, pause, take a moment, and listen to the spirit within. There, I often find the consolation I need and the answers I am seeking.

I am sure you have been at a crossroads in your life, even many. You have asked yourself which direction to take. Many people pass right through the crossroads without hesitation and move forward at a rapid pace. The wise person has learned to stop and consider their options, the dangers, and the directives from God's Word.

The Psalmist implores us to "Be Still" at moments such as these. We should listen for the voice of God speaking to our unique situation. When we do this, we find consolation for the journey. You may encounter emotions such as fear, anger, confusion, or grief at the crossroads, and you will need clear and sound directions before continuing forward. If we allow these emotions to win and overwhelm us, however, we may just lose sight of our destination.

We are encouraged to stop just long enough to receive that fresh message from God, never longer than necessary. There are choices that we must make, and they should be done after prayerful consideration of God's will.

Sometimes we just need to stop and look at the bigger picture of our lives—the implications of moving forward, turning, or even going back.

At any rate, we all need to occasionally stop and gain a new perspective on where we are going. I like the poet, Robert Frost, and especially his poem, "The Road Less Traveled." In the poem, he describes coming upon two roads in some wood. One was well-traveled, and the other was merely a path. He tells us that he took the path less traveled, and it made all the difference in his life.

My question to you is this: Will the road you are on get you to where you are going? If not, then any road will get you there!

We should all practice the art of stopping occasionally and praying over our situation. You will be surprised at the answers you will receive.

Some people seem to sit too long and let life pass them by. For example, I just preached Sunday about the four leprous men who sat at the city gate for days, weeks, or even longer, begging for handouts. The scripture is found in II Kings 7 and verse 3. It poses the same question to each of us in our situation:

"Why sit we here until we die?" (II Kings 7:3, KJV)

Their dilemma was pitiable. Leprosy was a devastating skin disease, and there would be no cure once contracted. Their city had recently been wrought with a terrible famine. People were dying inside the city walls, and no relief was in sight. The city was also under siege by a Syrian army, which had camped in the valley below.

Think of their terrible situation:

Their city was under siege.

Their food supply is exhausted.

Their leprosy and physical pain were unbearable.

Here are their only three options:

    1. Enter the city, and the famine will destroy them.

    2. Continue to sit where they were and die a slow death.

    3. Go out to the Syrian army, and they will be killed.

The lepers chose the latter. In what must have been excruciating pain, they walked the long road into the valley and entered the Syrian camp. This would have to be the darkest night of their lives! Instead, as they entered the camp, they found it empty. The army had left, and they had a complete run of the camp. Food was abundant, and gold and silver were everywhere! What a take when they had surely expected death. God had provided for them.

It was God who created the sound of many chariots, which caused the Syrian army to flee their camp. It was God, and not a stroke of luck, that provided the lepers with their first meal in days. It is God who constantly meets each of us at the point of our deepest need and makes a way out. He is at the crossroads of our lives, waiting.

"Be still and know that I am God."

One of the revelations we take from the story is how God cares for four leprous men whom society has shunned and excommunicated from the city. They had been left for dead at the city gate, hopeless and desperate. When God meets us at the point of our greatest need, we call it grace. When a judge gives a pardon to a guilty person, that is grace. Grace goes ahead of us and meets us at the crossroads. Grace provides a way out and directions for the weary traveler. Grace abounds when hope seems lost. God's grace provides!

I authored a book several years ago entitled *Lessons Learned from the School of Hard Knocks* (available on Amazon.com). In the book, I expose several events in my life that seemed hopeless at the time. However, in every situation, God made a way out, through, or around the problem until it was resolved. In each situation, I learned invaluable lessons about God's grace and his constant pursuit of us. The hardest lessons of life are learned at the point of God's grace. We are all in the "School of Hard Knocks."

Saint Augustine said, "The heart is restless, and it will not rest until it finds its rest in God." He had been to the same school as many of us. He learned there, through the same grace of God, that there is no peace, no rest for the weary soul, until it is experienced through God's amazing grace.

Mary Oliver said, "You can have all the other words - chance, luck, coincidence, serendipity. I'll take grace. I don't know what it is exactly, but I will take it."

Aberjhani said, "Un-winged and naked, sorrow surrenders its crown to a throne called grace."

What do you do and where do you turn when confronted with sorrow, fear, or desperation? When you stand at the crossroads or sit at the city gate, where do you look for hope? Who will save you? Who will lighten your weary load?

May I suggest that you turn to the "crown of grace?" Jesus is our greatest teacher and will never leave nor forsake us in our moments of greatest need.

So, if you are sitting at the city gate and life seems hopeless, arise, go to the crossroads, and find there, in Christ, rest for your weary soul!

LIFE'S LITTLE EXTRAS

Ever notice those little annoying inconveniences that come just when you are at your busiest? I have come to refer to them as "life's little extras." They happen when we least expect them. Unexpectedly, we are bombarded with an event that can change the entire course of our day. They can ruin even the best laid plans.

During a remarkably busy day, my son called from school with an upset stomach. I quickly changed my plans and rushed to the school to pick him up. Two hours later, unbelievably, my daughter called from junior high school with a splitting headache. As I picked her up with my son in tow, I wondered what else could happen.

Just an hour after taking the children home, my wife arrived from work with a terrible headache. Oh Boy! I guess it all worked for the good, however, for I would be leaving in a few minutes to participate in a funeral service for a loved one. I had Boy Scouts afterwards and a men's church supper following that. A lady was scheduled to come by after supper and talk with me about joining our church this Sunday. And... I must have this and three other articles in by morning to the newspaper for my weekly column.

And the beat goes on. Life is exciting around here, to say the least, especially with those little extras tacked on! But isn't that life? We learn to take it as it comes, or we fall apart in the process.

In 'Alexander and the Terrible, Horrible, No Good, Very Bad Day," Judith Viorst sums up my feelings about this kind of day I have had. Will there be other days like this? You bet 'cha! Suddenly, often without notice, plans change, and priorities must be shifted to accommodate those little extras. We must live flexible lives, always in tune with those little extra's life can and will throw in our way.

God can make those extras seem a bit more bearable if we only trust Him to work them out for us. We must be willing vessels in those frustrating moments to receive God's direction and leadership. In all things, He will make a way.

If we will stop and listen, God will speak to us amid our busy storm and remind us that He has everything under control. No need to fret or worry. God is in charge!

As my mother always said, "It will all come out in the wash, Charles!" Isn't that Good News for us today? I do not know the origin of that old saying, but it has always proven true: "The main thing is to keep the main thing the main thing!" God is the main thing! God bless you and have a great and interesting day.

That Sense of "Lostness"

Everywhere I look today, people seem lost in a kind of moral and spiritual "fog." They may be professing Christians, loving mothers and fathers, or even responsible citizens, but they also have a tremendous feeling of helplessness in the face of our constantly shifting values.

Jesus understood our feelings of lostness and helplessness. In the fifteenth chapter of Saint Luke's gospel, we read about three of His parables: a lost sheep, a lost coin, and a lost boy. He indicated in these parables that our lostness is of grave concern to the One who created us. In each parable, He shows us a way by which the lost may be found.

Let us consider, for a moment, our own current sense of lostness. While doing so, let us ask three basic questions:

    1. How did we get into this predicament?

    2. Does anyone really care?

    3. Is there an answer to our lostness or loneliness?

I believe our feelings of lostness can be linked directly to our "declining faith." We have simply lost faith in humanity today. Who do we look to in such circumstances? Our heroes are gone. We must turn to the only sure and sincere hope of our salvation—Jesus Christ! Our trust must be firmly placed in Him if we hope to be released from the doldrums of life.

The great tragedy of our lives is that, along with our declining faith in people, there has been a corresponding decline in our faith in God. Many people prefer their lostness! God forbid! Turn back to God, who cares for you and deeply loves you. You are the crowning work of His creation.

My question to you is this: If you cannot find Christ, then who is lost? You will always find Him right where you left Him. He is as close to you as your next breath.

The lost sheep was a good sheep, but it had wandered away from the flock and could not find its way back to the sheepfold. The shepherd went looking for the lost sheep until it was found and brought safely back to the fold. The shepherd called in all his friends and neighbors and celebrated the sheep's return by throwing a party! There was much rejoicing.

The lady with the lost coin searched high-and-low in her home until she found it. She had only ten coins of small worth, and that one coin was very vital and important to her subsistence. She lit a candle and searched everywhere until it was found. Then she called upon her family and friends to come celebrate her finding the coin.

My favorite of these three parables is the lost son, whom we always refer to as "the prodigal son." He was a good kid, but a bit misguided. He wanted to leave home and experience life outside of his big brother and his father. So, he takes his share of his inheritance, goes to a faraway country, and spends all of it. He soon finds himself slopping hogs in a pigpen for a local farmer. He is broken and destitute and begins to dream of a home where everything has been given to him. Coming to his senses one day, he decides to go back home and take whatever punishment is coming to him for leaving.

While returning home, his father meets him down the lane and hugs him with delight. He calls for the big brother to kill a fatted calf, for they were going to celebrate the son who had been lost and now found!

Do you not understand the parables? The Good Shepherd is Jesus; we are the lost sheep. Jesus is the woman with the lost coin who searches until it is found. The Good Father is Jesus, who always welcomes each of his children home again and celebrates when we are found.

There are none who are beyond being found and restored to the Father. He will always make a way for us to come home and will celebrate our reunion. Come to Jesus today and experience the good life!

Kathy's Letter

By Kathy Barron, (8-31-1953 - 8-27-2022)

Hi, family and friends.

If this letter is being read today,

Then I made my way to Paradise.

Today, as I walk through the Pearly Gates of Heaven,

I am renewed, restored, and healed.

No tears, no pain, just unspeakable joy!

I have lived a most wonderful life

Knowing Jesus on a very personal level.

I am saved by His amazing grace.

The journey has been long and

I never lost faith in my Lord and Savior.

He opened the gates of Heaven to me,

Saying those words that I wanted to hear -

"Welcome Home my good and faithful servant."

Death is not an ending. It is a transition from

Our earthly life to our eternal life.

Today, I am happy. I have no regrets, even after

The poor decisions I made for I learned

From them and grew from them.

I was never perfect, but I loved Jesus with my

Whole heart, soul, and spirit.

My dear ones, make sure that you know Jesus,

That you love Him, trust Him, and

That He has your heart and soul!

I pray that we will all meet again in this

Beautiful, magnificent paradise!

I must go for now, for this is a busy place

And I have much to do.

Remember to love, laugh, and

Be kind to one another.

I LOVE YOU ALL!

This letter was read at Kathy's graveside at her interment and was written by her prior to her passing. Permission for reprint granted by her husband, David Barron.

My COVID Dilemma

Following the great surge of COVID infections across America in the spring of 2020, Renee and I heeded all the warnings from the CDC (Centers for Disease Control) to protect us from getting the dreaded virus. We received our first available vaccines, bought boxes of masks, and practiced social distance everywhere, including our church. Numbers were increasing nationwide and around the world. People were dying in alarming numbers while the U.S. President and his party did their best to downplay the virus. Churches, restaurants, and factories were closing nationwide. Some of these would not reopen. I remember making toilet paper runs in all the stores that were open to secure a storehouse of supplies. These would be sold as quickly as the trucks rolled in! We saw very few people, and our social lives were lacking for months.

Then, I caught COVID! The day before, Renee had been hospitalized with a bad bout of pancreatitis. Due to my COVID infection, I could not go to the hospital and be with her. We communicated by phone and tried to commiserate with each other, but it was most difficult. My pharmacist saved my life by giving me some potent cough syrup and some great migraine-relieving pills, and I began slowly getting better. During its height, I was hurting from head-to-toe and felt miserable.

Finally, my physician sent me to the hospital to receive intravenous antibodies. I began feeling much better in the hours to come. The following day, I tested negative and began my five-day quarantine at home—alone! Two days later, I went to the hospital to pick up Renee, and we struggled together at home in isolation, but together. It was a terrible time, not just for us but for the entire world! Places of business would eventually reopen, and we could again procure items we needed.

Two years removed, and guess what? I have COVID again! I assume I picked it up at church because 10 others also contracted it that day from someone who was a carrier. This stuff is terrible! So, it is back to the antibiotics, cough syrup, and a ton of other medications my doctor prescribed. That was Tuesday, and on Saturday, Renee began having COVID symptoms as well! We bought a test, and she was positive! Can we please get a break here? My daughter, Angie, and her daughter, Meghan, have also contracted COVID!

Two weeks later, Renee is still testing positive. I cannot return to the pulpit to preach because I am at home with her and a potential carrier. I would never go to my church that way, exposing others to the virus.

Well, in a few days, our lives will return to normal, and we can get back into the groove of things. I miss my church, the fellowship, the preaching and singing, and the atmosphere. I am ready for my family to be healed from COVID!

The Capacity to Care

Pablo Casels said, "The capacity to care is the thing that gives life its deepest meaning and significance." When we invest our time, effort, and energy in helping others, we are always blessed in return. It gives our lives more meaning when we reach out to others in need.

There are people living on the fringes of society who are indigent, broken, and alone. Some are only a dollar away from complete poverty. Many do not eat the simple basics of food to maintain good health. Their children are also mixed into the equation and suffer greatly.

I have, on occasion, encountered such poor souls in my ministry and offered any help that I, or the church I was serving at the time, could lend. One such occasion follows.

I was visiting our local hospital one day, and a nurse, who knew me, asked if I could visit an elderly couple, Gloria and Jim, in the room next door. She told me that Jim had terminal cancer, and they did not have any health insurance, nor a pastor. The wife, Gloria, had requested the hospital chaplain or a local pastor to visit them. I promised her that I would check into their room, offer whatever help I could, and, at least, pray with them. His wife, Gloria, was also destitute and had profoundly serious heart problems.

Upon entering their room, I announced who I was, walked up to the bedside, and began a conversation. They were truly kind and welcoming, and I began asking what I could do for them as a pastor and new friend. Gloria asked if I could pray for them. She said that they were unchurched but believed in God and His ability to heal.

The woman's clothes were in tatters, and she appeared unkempt. The man was in a hospital gown and seemed fearful. He spoke truly little. I asked him what his doctor had told him about his condition, and he said that things looked bad. His cancer had returned after a two-year hiatus, and this time it had taken over his vital bodily functions. He was in excruciating pain. Gloria said, "Preacher, I don't know what I will do if he leaves me!" her voice trembling as she spoke.

I did my best to bring some semblance of comfort to them, but they were both crying when I asked them to join me in prayer. I held his other hand, and the three of us prayed. I prayed with all my heart that God would bring relief to the man and give him great peace and comfort. I then asked about their faith, and both said they believed in Jesus Christ. They asked if I would be their pastor, and I assured them that I would be honored. I told them that I would be back the following morning to check on them. I gave them my phone number and said they could call me anytime, day or night, if they needed me. They both thanked me and seemed a bit relieved after our time together.

I was called to the hospital at 10:30 p.m. that night from the nurse's station, and the nurse said the couple had requested my presence, if possible. I assured the nurse that I would be there in just a few minutes.

When I entered their room, Jim was writhing in excruciating pain. The nurse was administering some sedation for him when I entered, and then she left. Gloria hugged me so tightly that I feared being unable to breathe. "Preacher, the doctor just left and told us that Jim would not make it through the night. Could you stay with us for a little while?"

I again assured her that I would, and she seemed relieved.

It was a very restless night. At 3:00 a.m., Jim reared up his head, looked around the room, took his wife's hand, and died! She asked if I would stay with them until the funeral home folks came for him. In the meantime, I gave him his final rites, asking God to receive him into glory. Gloria made an unusual request at that point. "Preacher, we've never been baptized, so would you baptize both of us now?"

I thought for a moment and then told her, "Gloria, I would be delighted." It would be the first time I had baptized a deceased person, but I took a cup and filled it with water. I then read appropriate scriptures dealing with baptism, stuck my fingers into the cup of water, and sprinkled it on Jim's head and then on Gloria's head. I then made the sign of a cross on Jim's forehead. I then prayed a prayer of consecration for the both of them.

I stayed until Robert Barnes came from the funeral home with his stretcher. He asked if Gloria and I could wait outside the room until he had Jim ready for transport. He later came out with Jim, covered in a sheet, and Gloria bent over one last time and kissed Jim on his forehead. It was a very moving moment, and I even began crying.

Robert had asked if Gloria could come to the funeral home the next day at 10 a.m. to make plans for Jim's funeral. She asked if I would go with her, and, of course, I agreed. Without any subsistence, I wondered if she would be able to pay for the funeral. Robert then told me that he knew the couple and was sure that it would be a state pauper's funeral.

Jim and Gloria lived on the fringes of our town in a small squatter shack. She had given me directions to the house before we left the hospital, and I was heartbroken when I first saw the house. I would never consider putting a family in that little clapboard house.

Jim had been a sharecropper with local farmers for years and had drifted with Gloria from town to town, never once settling down for any extended period. They had no social security or any other means of income, so she would be unable to pay for the funeral. It was so sad.

Gloria came out of the house in what I figured was her best dress, and we left together for the funeral home. She also had some well-worn clothes for the funeral home to put on Jim for his burial. When there, Robert explained to her that the state allocated enough money for indigents who were to be buried, and Jim could be buried in the pauper's portion of the local cemetery.

He then asked for the listing of family members or pallbearers. Neither had family members, no children, and no one to call as pallbearers. Robert told her that they would take care of that part and not to worry.

Robert then led us into the casket room, where I could see beautiful, ornate caskets at the entrance and, further in the back, caskets designed to bury indigents. Robert went straight to the most popular hard-board casket and suggested it to Gloria. She agreed and asked me, "Preacher, don't you think this one (the casket) is fine?" I agreed, with my heart breaking again.

Jim was buried with a Christian funeral in the pauper's cemetery the next morning. I was there to do the eulogy, scripture readings, and prayers, along with the committal at the end. The funeral home staff carried his casket, with me helping. I had never helped to carry a casket before and never realized how heavy it was.

Gloria and I stood and watched the grave-digging crew cover his casket with sod and pat it down. After that, I led her to my car, and we drove to her house. Before leaving, I asked if we could do anything for her, and she said that she would appreciate a few groceries. I called a few of my church members, and they organized a group to purchase and carry groceries to her house that afternoon. She was so appreciative of everything.

I looked up from the pulpit that Sunday morning and saw my regular attendees along with one additional visitor. It was Gloria who sat in the back pew for the entire service. During the altar call service, Gloria came down, took my hand in hers, and kneeled for prayer.

Before I could begin a prayer, Gloria started praying in an extremely sweet and gentle voice: "Oh, God, healer of the brokenhearted, hear my prayer of thanksgiving for these good people of Christ Church who were sent by you to bring healing to Jim and myself. Bless them, Father, I pray."

I shared a few thoughts with her at the end of the service and told her that I would see her in a day or so to see if she needed further help.

I went by her little house two days later, and the house was completely empty. It was like she never existed. I had even begun to wonder if she was not an angel in disguise, sent to remind me of God's calling upon my life.

I never saw Gloria again, but I have gone by Jim's grave several times through the years and offered a prayer to God for him and Gloria, praying that God would keep her wherever she was and bless her.

We all need the capacity to care, without which we remain cold, callous, and broken. I met the face of God once again with Jim and Gloria in the hospital. I will never forget that event in my life. We must care for those on the fringes of our society, for "there by the grace of God go you and I."

Call Waiting

We receive calls daily on our cellphones or landlines. There are distinct types of calls, such as telemarketers, family members, friends, doctor's offices, etc. We are constantly bombarded with such calls. Many of them we anticipate, but others become a pain to answer.

Renee and I recently dropped our landline because the only calls we were receiving daily were from telemarketers. They announced such things as me having won the Publisher's Clearing House two-million-dollar sweepstakes! Their voices were always those of an Indian from India who spoke extremely poor English. All I would have to do would be to go to my local Walmart and purchase a gift card for $299 to pay for the expenses of shipping my sweepstakes check to me! How ludicrous! You would be surprised, however, at how many people fall for the scheme and blow that $299. No matter how many times we would contact our local phone company to remove such calls, we still received them, sometimes late at night after we had gone to bed! We finally decided to survive only with our cellphones and get rid of the landline.

Calls are constant. We may choose to answer them or just ignore them.

In the biblical book of I Samuel:3, we encounter an old prophet, Eli, and his young protege, Samuel. God began calling out to young Samuel in his sleep one night, and he assumed that it was Eli. calling. When he awakened Eli and asked if he had called, Eli assured him that he had not. He was told to go back to bed. He did, but shortly afterwards, Samuel heard the voice again. This happened three times until Eli realized that it must have been God calling young Samuel. He told Samuel to go back to bed and, if he heard the call again, he should answer the Lord, "Speak, for thy servant heareth." (I Samuel 3:10 KJV). It only took three times for Samuel to finally answer.

How many times has God called you, friend? The truth is that He calls regularly, but we are often too busy to hear His voice. We are preoccupied with so many things in our lives that a voice from God does not resonate. I have found that you hear what you listen to.

For example, a friend shared with me years ago that his brother had gone to New York City for a visit with his sister. He was from South Georgia and had gone walking down Park Avenue with his sister one day when, suddenly, he heard a cricket chirping somewhere along the street. When he asked his sister if she could hear it, she acted as if he was crazy. "Are you kidding me?" she responded. "No, I distinctly heard a cricket chirping!" he replied.

His sister then responded by asking how he could hear a simple little cricket when the traffic zooming by was so loud and street workers were pounding away at concrete on the sidewalk.

"I guess you hear what you want to hear, Sis!" he said. And we are no different. In the busyness of life, we are all bombarded with sounds of all kinds. The key is to be focused on those "other" sounds that may be of import to us.

During the early years of having our first child, I recall Renee being so overly sensitive to even the slightest noise from our baby in the other room. The baby made little sounds that I could not hear, but her mother could hear her distinctly. We hear what we listen for.

God was speaking to young Samuel and calling him to respond. At first, without Eli's recourse, Samuel had no idea that it could be God, for he had no relationship with him at the time. Once Eli told the boy to return to bed and respond on the third attempt by God, Samuel could then distinctly hear the voice of God calling.

I also love the beautiful discourse God has with Elijah in I Kings 19. Elijah was being threatened by Queen Jezebel, so Elijah fled into the wilderness, where he prayed in earnest for his life. There, an angel appeared to him and gave him strength with food and water. Elijah then travels forty days and nights to reach the mountain of God in Horeb. While there, the Lord appeared to Elijah in three distinct forms on the mountain. A strong wind came, and then an earthquake. Following that, a fire came, but Elijah did not see God in any of those calamitous events. Then came a very gentle whisper: "What are you doing here, Elijah?"

Finally, Elijah recognized the voice of God, and it was not in the wind, the earthquake, or the fire, but in a very gentle whisper. If you are looking for God in the miraculous things and events of life, you may fail to find him. He is as close to you as your next breath. Hear Him and respond.

In Psalms 139, David says, "Lord, you have searched me and known me. . . Thou hast laid thine hand upon me. . . Where shall I go to escape from thee?" (Psalm 139:1-7 KJV) We cannot hide from the Lord's presence, for He is always near us. Whether we recognize His presence is another matter.

David again reiterates the importance of waiting on the Lord in Psalms 46:10: "Be still and know that I am God." (KJV) Too often, in our busyness, we fail to hear that small voice of God speaking in our midst. Too often, we ignore His signs and wonder about ourselves. David knew the importance of being still and listening to the voice of God. God had led him through many trials and tribulations and brought him to greatness in the end.

And of course, there is that beautiful Psalm of David (Chapter 23), in which David recognizes God as the one who leads him through the valley of the shadow of death and brings him safely to the other side. When we recognize God as our substance and strength, we will prosper and grow in our relationship with Him.

In I Corinthians 6:12-20 (KJV), the Apostle Paul gives a discourse on patience and waiting on the Lord. In verse 12, we read, "All things are lawful unto me, but all things are not expedient... I will not be brought under the power of any." He mentions food in verse 13 but states that food is not the total of our sustenance. In verse 19, we read that our bodies make up the temple of God. Our bodies are holy and designed for the purposes of God and should be treated as such. Paul calls us to "glorify" God in all things, in every situation.

I recently read an article about a popular rock star who states that God has been calling him to seek more alone time and silence in his personal life and listen to Him more. He now feels that he should just be quiet and listen to what God is trying to say to him. He advises us that we should perhaps take our faith to the next level and actually spend time rethinking our lives. He no longer seeks to return home again because he feels that home is actually not a place but a person, and that person is God.

I detest calling a doctor's office and being put on call waiting, don't you? What about God's call on your life? Have you put Him on call waiting? Why not rethink your life and discover that home is not a place but a person? Your life will take on new meaning and purpose when you do. Hear that small voice calling today and find your way home.

Going Where the Fish Are

An elderly member of a church I served years ago took me fishing early one morning and taught me a very valuable lesson in preparation. I had gone to Walmart a few days before and had stocked up on the latest lures, line, and other tackle for the trip. I wanted to impress my friend and show him how prepared I was with all the latest gadgets. To my surprise, he opened his tackle box and had only two lures in it, both appearing to be very old and well-used. He did not seem impressed with my cache of shiny new lures and the apparent price that I had paid for them.

"Preacher, we are not out here this morning to impress anyone but these bass," he said. We loaded our rod-and-reels and tackle boxes into the John boat, and my friend maneuvered it into a small cove, where we dropped anchor. It was 6:30 a.m., and mist had enveloped the swampy area where we were fishing. There was a coolness in the air, and, of course, I had not dressed accordingly! I began to feel like a heel in the presence of this seasoned fisherman.

As we sat there in the cove, I began casting my line like crazy. My son had taught me to fish in a circular motion from left to right. As I cast for the tenth time, my friend told me, "Be patient, preacher. Do not reel in your line so quickly. It's early, so give the bass a fighting chance."

My friend soon caught a largemouth bass that probably weighed around five pounds. I was impressed, especially watching as he released that beautiful fish back into the cove! I grew up fishing out of necessity, so we kept everything we caught in ponds, rivers, or creeks. After he caught a couple more fish, he decided to pull up the anchor and move us to another cove. He then said, "Preacher, I'm taking you to my honey hole." A honey hole is a name for a spot where anglers know big bass hang out.

We went around a few cypress trees growing up in the water, and he found the honey hole in a few minutes. To me, it really looked fishy. Steam was coming up from the water, and the sun was beginning to rise.

Within a few minutes, my friend had hung another big bass and seemed to be struggling a bit to reel him in. As soon as I saw the fish coming up out of the water, I asked my friend, "What's your secret? I've used several lures already to no success." He then opened his tackle box, took out his second lure, and handed it to me. "Put this on your line, Preach, and you'll catch a bass."

I rigged my line with his old, dilapidated lure. It looked as if several big bass had left their teeth marks on the outside of the lure through the years.

He pointed me to a section of the cove and told me to cast there. "When it lands on the water, let it sink a little and slowly bump your line and reel slowly as well," he said.

As soon as that old lure hit the water, something struck my line with great force! I jerked back on my line and banged! I had a fish! I reeled it in with the exhilaration of having finally caught a fish. "Take your time. He's not going anywhere," he said.

A three-pound bass was on the other end of my line, and I was laughing as I reeled him in. My excitement was apparent. I thanked my friend for the use of his lure, and he said, "That's now your lure, Preach."

I let the bass go and cast again. Boom! Another bass struck my lure and I reeled him in. That scenario happened several more times before the morning ended, and we loaded up and left the lake.

I learned some very valuable lessons that day. It boils down to this: location, knowing where the fish are, having the right tackle (regardless of its age), and then how to bring them in once you've hung them. My old friend knew exactly where the fish would be and what it would take to catch them. Preparation and patience always pay a dividend in life and fishing.

Jesus once called his disciples to follow him, and he would make them fishers of men. In order to lead people to the Savior, one must prepare, be patient, and persevere through it all until the right bait is used to lure that soul into the kingdom. It does not take rocket science to learn how to catch bass, and it does not take all of the latest fads and frills to lure a lost world to Christ. Loving people, showing them you really care, and bringing them to the Lord is the right stuff to use. It does not take new fangled tactics, but good old common sense, love, and the willingness to go where the fish are!

Soft Landings and Smooth Flights

I recently passed a church that had a sign on its marquee that read, *God always promises a soft landing, but he never promises a smooth flight!* The saying reminded me of a flight I was on several years ago while on a mission trip.

Our team had been in the Amazon region of southern Venezuela for ten days while working on a mission church. We had all said our goodbyes to the locals of the church on our final day and headed for the airport with our luggage in tow. The airport was very small and situated on the Columbian border with Venezuela. Our expected flight was to pick us up after arriving from Bogota, Columbia, and carry us on to our connection in Caracas. The plane never arrived due to inclement weather over the Andes mountains. So our team had to spend the night at the airport and was promised another flight in the morning. We had not taken baths, so we were joking with each other about weird smells in our midst!

Finally, our flight the next morning arrived very early, and we were loaded with our luggage and team members on a rustic-looking puddle jumper! We flew directly over the Andes on our way to Caracas. It was the worst flight of my life! The inclement weather caused many updrafts, and we would dip very low and then rise up high again all the way to Caracas. The old DC-3 plane bounced, tilted from side to side, and swayed off course several times. I did more praying during that trip than I had previously prayed in all the churches I have served.

At the Caracas airport, we had already missed our connecting flight to Miami, and there were no other flights available until the next morning. However, this time, the airline did put us up for the night in a local motel, so we got some much-needed rest.

The following morning, we were finally able to catch a flight to Miami. We were tired, late, and very weary. Storms were brewing all over the Miami airport area, and so we had to circle the airport for around 45 minutes until we were able to land. Lightning was striking everywhere!

After our Miami arrival, we learned that our next flight would be around 6 p.m. that evening, so we had a five-hour layover again in the airport. Delays, due to the stormy weather, pushed our departure time to 7:30 p.m. We were then given the O.K. to take off on one of those little American airlines that held about 30 people. We would have to fly across Florida to the Tampa airport and then on to the Tallahassee airport, where our church van was, for our return trip home. From Miami, we were bounced around several times on our way to Tampa. Before landing in Tampa, the pilot notified us on the intercom that the weather was very bad at the airport and there may be delays before landing. Oh, boy, here we go again! What else could go wrong on this trip? As I looked out my window during our approach to the Tampa airport, I noticed all of the lightning around the plane. I began praying in earnest that God would bring us down safely. The pilot began his ascent to the airport, and just before touching down, he immediately pulled the plane back up again and started circling the airport! On the intercom, he let us know that everything was fine. He would just have to circle a couple more times, but we would land in just a few more minutes. I then invited all 30 people on that plane to join hands with someone near them as I led us all in a prayer. Before I completed the prayer, the plane touched down on the runway and brought us to the terminal. Whew! What a trip!

From Tampa, we had a two-hour layover until another plane was scheduled to take us to Tallahassee. Our mission team was so weary and worn and had been through a lot. We said a prayer together before boarding our Delta flight to Tallahassee, and the flight was a smooth breeze! Thank you, Lord.

It goes to show you that even a mission team doing the Lord's work in a foreign country has to go through some bumpy rides occasionally to accomplish what needs to be done. God bless those souls who travel to Africa, across Europe, and Central and South America to bring the gospel and work of Christ to the masses. Their names may never be recorded in the annals of history, but they are precious souls to me.

None of us are immune to these kinds of events in life, but we can always rest in the knowledge that we are never alone on our journey. God's word promises that He will always be with us, and there will be a soft landing!

Keep the faith, my dear friend. The journey ahead may become a bit bumpy, but you'll make it.

Right Where You Left Him

Our mission team was touring Versailles, France, just outside Paris, at the completion of our mission. While inside that palatial palace, we began to realize that one of our team members had strayed from the group. Hundreds of people were filtering around through room after room, so it was easy for one to become lost in the crowd. Directions and a map had been given to each of us, just in case one became lost. I had told our team that if they became lost, they were to meet us just outside the gift shop at the end of the tour.

So we divided the team into partners when we realized that this one lady was missing. They were to go back through the crowds of people looking for our member. After everyone had searched through the mansion, we all met at the gift shop. Our lost member was nowhere to be found!

Finally, one member suggested that we check back at the tour bus for her, and there she was! I nearly lost my temper at that point, but she remembered me telling the team that they could also return to our tour bus if they finished the tour early. She told us that she was exactly where she should have been. Needless to say, I kept my eye on that member throughout the rest of our trip!

We've all strayed from God, even during those times when we just knew we were exactly where He wanted us to be. Yet, God wanted us in a different place. Staying in touch with God through prayer and commitment always helps us be where He wants us to be. To become lost in other interests will certainly lead us away from God's will. We must learn to stay on course.

I love the story of Jesus in Luke 2. Jesus was twelve at the time and was left behind in Jerusalem at the end of Passover week by his parents. After an entire day's journey on their way back home, they realized that their son was missing. They would make another day's journey back to Jerusalem to find their son, eventually finding him in the temple, right where they had left him!

Have you lost God? Have you strayed from His tender love, mercy, and grace? Want to find Him again? Well, you will, if you search for Him with all your heart, soul, mind, and strength.

Guess what? He'll be right where you left Him!

Horse Creek and Other Near Calamities

On several occasions, when I confronted death head-on, I was able to evade it by the grace of God.

When I was five years old, our dad took my two brothers and me to Sugar Creek one day to teach us how to swim. My middle brother Robert could swim well, and he immediately jumped in, but my oldest brother, Raymond, and I just stood on the bank watching Robert. My dad came over and grabbed me, threw me into the water, and said, "Swim, son!" I thought he had a very warped idea as to how to teach a child to swim! My brother Raymond came to my rescue and pulled me out of the water just in time to prevent my drowning. He was my first encounter with grace.

I was traumatized from that day forward, and I never trusted my dad again. I felt that he did not have my best interests at heart.

My next encounter with grace came when I was eight years old. I call it my "Coca-Cola Pond" experience. While fishing next to my brother Raymond one day, I slipped into the deep water of that pond and began struggling to find the bank. I was going under for the third time when Raymond grabbed my arms and pulled me up on the bank to safety. Had it not been for him, I would certainly have drowned.

At twelve, I walked the railroad tracks to the trestle, which spanned the Little Ocmulgee River. I was with two neighborhood friends that day, and they were both good swimmers. Once we reached the trestle, they both jumped off the trestle (about 15 feet) into the river below. They kept shouting at me to jump in, but I refused and told them that I would just wait there on the trestle.

Before long, they decided to come back up to the trestle. They grabbed me against my will and threw me off the trestle into the river. I began drowning, and they saw me struggling and jumped in to save me.

Near my home, a brand-new public pool had opened. I went with my friend Donnie one night to check it out. After climbing over the fence, we stripped down to our underwear. Naturally, I found myself at the shallow end of the pool, while Donnie dove headfirst into the deep end. Eventually, I made my way around to the deep end of the pool. The wet pavement caused me to slip and fall into the water. To my good fortune, or divine providence, I was able to make it to the edge of the pool on my first attempt. Grace, a stranger, miraculously rescued me once more.

The very next year, Donnie and his uncle, along with my other friend, Charles, took a trip one Sunday afternoon to Horse Creek to fish, swim, and explore the woods. Horse Creek had a pooled-up area where people had been swimming for years. There was also a swing rope tied to a tree limb, which people used to swing out over the pooled area and drop off to swim. Donnie and Charles started swinging out and dropping into the pool several times while I waited with Donnie's uncle on the bank. We were both fishing downstream, away from the noise.

Before long, Donnie and Charles came and encouraged me to come jump in with them. They assured me that the water in the pool was only a few feet deep and that I would be all right.

As soon as I swung out over the pool and dropped into the water, I panicked and started taking in water. Donnie realized that I was in distress, so he came to me and pulled me up to the sandbar for safety. It was another act of grace. Another disaster was avoided.

I can still vividly recall going canoeing in Stone Mountain State Park Lake in Atlanta, even after all these years have passed. The purpose of the trip was to assist my Boy Scout troop in gaining various merit badges, such as those for canoeing, swimming, and conservation. We rented five canoes and started off across the lake with two young men in each canoe. Because we were all wearing life vests, I was not concerned about my safety. In order to return the canoes after we had finished our work, we proceeded back to the shore. About 10 feet off the shoreline, one of those scouts used his paddle to shove my boat over. As soon as the young men became aware that I was in danger, they turned the canoe over and assisted me in getting to the shore. I had been trapped underneath the canoe, so the boys saved my life!

To summarize, I have always had a deep respect for water and a deep dread of it when I was younger. However, I have never been the type of guy who would jump in and start swimming right away, and I have always respected those who are able to do so.

While I was attending Emory University in Atlanta for the first week of my seminary studies, my wife called me from home, three hours away. My brother Raymond had gone missing in a creek, and the Civil Defense had been called in to drag the creek for him. I quickly made my way home to be with my wife and mother.

During that afternoon, Raymond had been fishing upstream when he became aware of a disturbance coming from downstream and dashed to investigate. While he was searching for the commotion, he came across a woman who was struggling to get her three-year-old daughter to the bank. After he had reached out and secured the child, he went back to try and fetch the mother. As soon as he had successfully rescued her from the perilous situation, he was thrown into the vortex. Because he had never learned how to swim, he began to drown and disappeared instantly beneath the whirlpools of water that were flowing down the creek. A couple of hours later, the Civil Defense unit found my brother using grappling hooks. The roots had entangled his garments, and he was unable to free himself from the situation. He was around thirteen feet down in the turbulent water. Even though he was able to save two lives, he was unable to save himself.

In addition to buying me candy many times, protecting me from bullies in the neighborhood, and rocking me when I was a newborn, my brother was the best brother anyone could wish for. And he was now gone—gone in such a short amount of time. He was able to save the lives of two people, but he was unable to rescue himself!

When I think back on my life, I am acutely aware of how fortunate I have been. When I was in the greatest need of assistance, God sent people to help me, and they have been one of the biggest blessings in my life. Someone came to my rescue each time I was at the point of drowning. My eyes have been opened to the fact that it was not merely a coincidence but rather God's plan for my life. Throughout all those challenging occasions, he was there for me, providing support to me no matter what the circumstances were. I am grateful for the wonderful grace and kindness that God has bestowed upon me, as well as for the exceptional people that he has sent. The fact that I am aware that He has a plan for my life gives me confidence that He will guide me through any obstacle that I encounter.

Grace is a person, whether it be a friend, stranger, or even God!

Assurances of the Christian Faith

There are thousands of words that give Christian believers assurances of faith. In this discourse, I will attempt to list a few of the major ones for you to meditate on, along with scripture references for further study. All scripture is from the King James Version (KJV) of the Holy Bible.

- **GRACE**: Romans 5:2 states, "By whom also we have <u>access</u> by <u>faith</u> into this <u>grace</u> wherein we stand and <u>rejoice</u> in <u>hope</u> of the <u>glory</u> of God." (Underlining emphasizes other words of assurance.)

The Apostle Paul states the way to salvation for us here in Romans. It was the first book I read as a new convert to Christianity at the age of seventeen. Verse 2 includes the words underlined above, which are also assurances of our faith.

Access: We have been given access to God through His Son, Jesus Christ, who gave his life willingly upon the cross, was resurrected from the tomb, and now sits at the right hand of God in glory. The way forward was prepared for us by Jesus.

Ephesians 2:18: "For through him we both have <u>access</u> by one <u>Spirit</u> unto the Father." Ephesians 3:12: "In whom we have <u>boldness</u> and <u>access</u> with <u>confidence</u> by the <u>faith</u> of him."

Do you see what happened in these two scriptures? Each passage lists more words of assurance for us. One scripture leads us to another, and each contains gems of our faith. It has been said that you can open your Bible to any passage and find such gems over and over again.

To me, grace was my wonderful 4th grade teacher, Mrs. Harris. She took a very incorrigible child (me) and gave me hope to become somebody. I had gotten into trouble one day on the playground by breaking a school window with a rock. I was sent to the principal's office, given a good spanking, and told that I would stay after school each day for one week with my teacher, Mrs. Harris. Each day, during that period, she would talk to me about life, responsibilities, and my duty to her and the other students to be the best I could be and not do harm. She knew my family and the dysfunctional way we lived, and she shared with me that I could be anything I wanted to be. I needed her and am grateful to this day for what she shared with me.

Grace was a juvenile court judge. At thirteen, I was arrested and given a sentence of one year in a juvenile detention center three hours from home. While awaiting my transport to the center, the judge who had sentenced me called me into the courtroom the day before Christmas and decided to put me on one year of probation. I was to meet weekly with a local minister for counseling. The judge told me that it was his policy to let someone go each year prior to Christmas, and I was most thankful and blessed.

That year of counseling with the minister helped pave the way for me to later enter the ordained ministry. The judge's decision also helped me secure a job at twenty years old as a community worker with the juvenile court system. I would do that job for almost three years and genuinely loved my work representing other kids like I had. I then entered fulltime ministry and have served churches for over 52 years! As I look back on all of this, I can only say that it was all because of God's grace and a broken window!

Grace was also the man at the check-out counter. He was ahead of me in line and did something quite unexpected. He paid for my groceries in advance. I did not realize what he was doing until I checked out, and the clerk notified me that my groceries had been paid for by the guy who checked out in front of me. By that time, he had left the store, and I had no idea who he was or how to thank him for such a wonderful thing. That was an undeserved grace! God supplies it to His children regularly.

Grace was also a precious little lady in my first church as pastor who encouraged me each week and complimented my crude attempts at preaching. She gave me much-needed guidance on how to properly conduct a worship service and how to talk to people about their faith. Her smile was always contagious and warm. Her voice was tender and soothing. That, again, was grace.

Back now to Romans. We read in Chapter Five and verse 8 (my favorite passage in scripture!) the following: "But God <u>commendeth</u> his <u>love</u> toward us, in that, while we were yet sinners, <u>Christ died for us</u>." In other words, God "showed" us what love is by sending His only Son to die for our sins. Our sins have been covered by the Lamb of God. Our indebtedness has been paid in full!

- **SANCTIFIED:** "And such were some of you: but ye are <u>washed,</u> but ye are <u>sanctified,</u> but ye are <u>justifie</u>d in the name of the Lord Jesus, and by the <u>Spir</u>it of our God." I Corinthians 6:11

I Thessalonians 5:23: "And the very God of <u>peace sanctify</u> you wholly; and I <u>pray</u> God your whole spirit, soul, and <u>body</u> be <u>preserved blameless</u> unto the coming of our Lord Jesus Christ."

From these two passages, we learn that those who have been saved by God's grace have been washed in the blood of Jesus, sanctified by God, and justified (set right) by the Father. Notice the second passage. God is the God of peace, never one of division, hatred, or confusion. He sanctifies us in spirit, soul, and body while preserving us blameless (although guilty through our sins).

I could go into more detail on any of these great assurances, but I'll leave that part of the study up to you. Do your homework.

- **ANOINTED:** This is a beautiful word and reminds me of Psalm 23:5. "Thou <u>preparest</u> a table before me in the presence of my enemies; thou <u>anointest</u> my head with oil; my <u>cup</u> runneth over."

David, the author of the Psalm, was first a shepherd. A shepherd cares for his sheep and looks after all their needs. He moves his flock from pasture to pasture to find the best food for them. In a similar fashion, God knows our needs long before we ask Him. A shepherd checks his sheep's condition regularly for sores, and if any exist, he prepares a soothing balm of ointment. He then applies the ointment to the affected sheep. In a similar fashion, God cares for us and supplies our needs.

- **COMFORT:** Just as a shepherd comforts his sheep, our Lord brings us the assurance of comfort in our hour of need.

Again, we read in Psalm 23:4, "Yea, though I walk through the valley of the shadow of death, I will fear no evil: for thou art with me, thy rod and thy staff they <u>comfort</u> me." God's promise is never to leave us. We have the assurance that He is always there, protecting us from evil. Even through dying, we have His assurance that He will see us through that valley and bring us to a place of comfort. The shepherd's staff protects his sheep from danger, or an enemy that seeks to attack the flock. We always have our Lord's protection.

- **REDEEMED:** We have been redeemed by the blood of Jesus. We do not deserve redemption, but Christ has opened the door for us through his death and resurrection. It has been given freely to those who will receive it. If I am given a free coupon for an item at the grocery store, I must take it to the merchant, pick up the product, and show the coupon to receive my discount. This is redemption in its purest sense.

Psalm 49:15: "But God will redeem my soul from the power of the grave; for he shall receive me."

Psalm 130:8: "And he shall redeem Israel from all his iniquities." Rejoice in the fact that God gives you a way out of every situation through His redemption. Cash in that coupon today and rejoice in your salvation.

- **TRIBULATION:** Why would I use this word as an assurance? Simply put, in this life, we will all have tribulations. We have not been made immune to it. In fact, because of our faith, we will be more persecuted and tried. We need to understand this assurance and what it offers the believer.

Romans 5:3: 'And not only so, but we glory in tribulations also, knowing that tribulations worketh patience."

Jesus, you recall, suffered a cruel and agonizing death on Calvary. Nails were driven through his hands and feet; he was beaten within a breath of dying; a sword pierced his side; and a bitter gall was administered to him for his wounds. The humiliation was more than you and I could take, yet He did it freely to gain our salvation. Our earthly tribulations (troubles and trials) are far less severe than the ones Christ endured.

We are humans, and we will endure tribulations in this life. We cannot and will not escape it. We must, therefore, learn to endure through all of it to become stronger in faith. It is tribulation, as the Apostle Paul says, that brings us patience. Patience is a particularly important virtue we must learn if we are to be faithful to God.

I detest doctor offices! My wife, Renee, usually goes with me to remind me to be patient. I rush about to get there before my appointed time, only to sit there for an hour or two before they call me back. They put me into a holding room where I sit for another half to one hour before someone comes in, either an N.P. (nurse practitioner) or a P.A. (physician's assistant). They quickly examine you and alert you that the doctor is not there that day! What? I kept this appointment because I needed to see the doctor, not an assistant! Renee tries to comfort me and reminds me to be patient. It is hard to do that, but we must.

If you are alive, you will endure tribulation. Be patient and faithful, and look to the Savior and the example He gave us on that cross.

This was not intended to be an exhaustive list of assurances, but a starting point for you. There are thousands of them in the scriptures. I have given you, hopefully, the impetus to dig deeper into the words of God and discover other gems like the ones below:

PEACE, BLESSED, CHOSEN

CHILDREN OF GOD, ACCEPTED

HOLY, LOVED, ADOPTED

FORGIVEN, TRUST, SEALED

PROMISE, HOPE, and Faith

POWER, GOOD WORKS, ORDAINED

RECONCILED, SPIRITUAL, FELLOW CITIZENS

HOLY TEMPLE, MERCY, HOLY GHOST

Look them up in your Bible and study each. You may even start a journal, begin with the first assurance, and put your understanding of it in your own words. You will be amazed at how your faith will grow and mature. God bless you on your journey.

Fruits of the Spirit

Christians hear a lot about the "fruits of the Spirit." Keep in mind that just as fruit trees are expected to produce fruit, so too are Christian believers. According to Galatians 5:22-23, the nine fruits we should bear are:

- LOVE, JOY, PEACE
- LONGSUFFERING
- GENTLENESS
- GOODNESS
- FAITH
- MEEKNESS
- TEMPERANCE

These nine should be self-explanatory. They should be exemplary for every believer and should be utilized in our daily lives. Christ is our ultimate example.

If I were you, I would commit these to memory and seek ways to live them out daily. God bless you on your journey.

A Spiritual Fork in the Road

> Romans 12:1,2: "I beseech you therefore, brethren, by the mercies of God, that ye present your bodies a living sacrifice, holy, acceptable unto God, which is your reasonable service. And be not conformed to this world: but be ye transformed by the renewing of your mind, that ye may prove what is that good, and acceptable, and perfect, will of God."

When you feel that you have arrived at a spiritual fork in the road, decisions may be difficult to make. The things of this world have clouded your mind, which is why it is not clear. Too many people offer their understanding and explanations of why things are as they appear. But you have been exposed to the king of Kings and the lord of Lords and you know which way you should travel. You stand there perplexed, examining each fork and what it might offer while considering the implications of choosing either. You were not made for this moment, but this moment was made for you! You must decide based on your knowledge and the grace of God. Years of preparation have gone into your decision, so choose wisely.

In Romans, Paul instructs the followers of God to be holy, blameless, and "acceptable unto God." They are to present themselves as sacrifices for the glory of God. They are not to conform to the things of this world but to be changed into the likeness of Christ. This is the bounden duty of a Christian, transformed by the power of God.

If you find yourself at a fork in the road and cannot seem to make up your mind as to which way to go, then simply take up your cross and follow Jesus. He always makes it possible for you to know yourself. The choice is eventually up to you.

As Christians we must bear our own cross daily. That includes tribulations, trials, or even forks in the road. When all signs say, "Follow Me" and one leads to destruction, it becomes an even harder task to bear. We must trust in the One who has already made that journey and decision - Jesus. In bearing our cross, I do not mean that we embrace sufferings or burdens without meaning for that would be absurdity. We therefore bear our crosses for the sake of Christ who died a cruel death for us on Calvary and showed the world a more excellent way to live.

To Christ, our lives are meaningful and significant and full of purpose. In him, we know who we are and whose we are! We belong to God and are counted as sheep in his fold. May we live in that victorious standing today and seek to become better Christians.

God bless you on your journey today.

Chapter 4
BIBLE TALKS FOR DAILY WALKS

(These are intended as guides for you to meditate on during your daily walks with God)

Filled With New Wine

Acts 2:13: "Others mocking said, These men are full of new wine."

Christians should be the happiest people on earth! We should be beacons of light that draw others to the Savior. But strangely, we are among the saddest people.

On the day of Pentecost, when the Holy Spirit fell upon the disciples of Jesus, they became jubilant, excited, and could not contain themselves! Those who witnessed their elation said they were "full of new wine." It was, of course, the Holy Spirit of God that had entered them. When the Spirit enters, we become new creatures. We walk differently, talk differently, and are full of God's love, almost as though we are drunk!

As a pastor, I have witnessed church members living such sullen and mundane lives. They accept their faith, but seldom live it out. The Spirit life is one of confidence, boldness, and exuberance. You would be hard-pressed today to find even one person like that in any local congregation.

Notice in 2:17-18, how the Spirit is poured out on those approximately 120 disciples (men and women) in Acts 1:15. They began speaking in foreign languages, prophesying, seeing visions, and dreaming dreams. Wonders began to occur, and miracles took place. Oh, for a church like that!

Imagine the impact if one church, no matter its size, became filled with this new wine. They could literally change the world around them. Others would soon flock to that church just to see what all the commotion was about.

My prayer today is that you will invite the Spirit of God to take residence in your heart. Once He does, get ready, for life will never be the same for you again.

God bless you all on your journey today. Be filled with new wine!

GIVING ALMS

Matthew 6:4: "That thine alms may be in secret: and thy Father which seeth in secret himself shall reward thee openly."

Whatever you give to God should be done in secret without telling the world about it. It is a very sacred thing between you and the Father. Being faithful in tithes and offerings has always been at the forefront of my ministry.

Renee and I were in our first pastorate, and we were both very busy with three small country churches while attending college at the same time. Furthermore, I had a job as a juvenile court worker during the week and attended night classes at college. While paying for college tuition, books, etc., each semester, there was not much money to spare for our other needs, but God gave the increase because of our faithfulness.

On one occasion, I recall being short of a hundred dollars that was due the following week. I had no resources to draw from and only twenty dollars in our bank account. I needed to pay that bill without going into arrears. So, Renee and I prayed about it and decided to give the twenty dollars in church that Sunday since it wasn't a hundred dollars.

On Tuesday of that week, as God is my witness, we received a letter with a check inside for $250. A note was included which read, "Just thought you could use this little bit of help. God bless you for what you are doing at our church." God was faithful to us and supplied our need. We were able to pay the $100 that week with plenty left over!

God is an abundant and gracious God to those who remain faithful. When we give our alms (tithes and offerings), we give, not expecting anything in return. We are simply being faithful to the God who gave everything to us and has promised to take care of our needs. Once again, God fulfilled his promises to us.

Being faithful and giving our tithes and offerings is just one of many ways to give alms to God. We also give of our time, talents and resources to others in various ways. Renee and I have visited nursing homes for years now, been on numerous mission trips abroad and at home, and have served our community in many capacities to make it better.

Remember that a tithe is one-tenth of our "gross" income. An offering is anything above and beyond that. Are you being a faithful alms giver?

Think of ways in which you may give more generously to your church or community. I am sure that you'll discover that God will greatly enrich your life and your pocketbook by doing His holy will!

God bless you on your journey today.

A Thicker-Thinner

Leviticus 17:11: "For the life of the flesh is in the blood: and I have given it to you upon the altar to make an atonement for your souls: for it is the blood that maketh an atonement for the soul."

My neighbor, David, is a wonderful fellow, a faithful father and husband, and works each day driving a dump truck for our county. It is tough work, but he really enjoys it. David has also had quite a bit of trouble with his heart lately, and the doctors are constantly trying different medications to bring his blood pressure down and thin his blood. It's a tight rope walk for David. He's been hospitalized on various occasions, and doctors have struggled to find the right prescriptions to work for him.

Recently, David shared with me that the doctor, who had given him a prescription for blood thinners, had now decided to give him a "thicker-thinner." The name confused me at first, but then it makes sense. It is a medication that prevents blood clots from forming and can be prescribed for heart disease, strokes, or even deep vein thrombosis.

It's all in the blood, isn't it? Blood has been a big subject throughout the Bible, and rightfully so. It was the blood of goats and rams upon the altar that gave forgiveness for sins to those in the Old Testament age. The blood of Jesus, shed upon the cross, provided our sin- covering. Without blood there would be no remission of sins. Thank God for the precious blood of Jesus.

I have given over three gallons of blood to the Red Cross over the years, but now, because of my heart condition, high blood pressure, and high cholesterol, I am unable to give any longer. I realize how very important those pints that I gave were to someone in need of a transfusion. In fact, I was given five pints of blood recently during a hospital stay while having bleeding varices in my esophagus. Someone had to give that blood to me, and I am most thankful!

If you will recall in the scripture above, "the life of the flesh is in the blood." The blood is the life-giving portion of our bodies, without which we would surely perish.

Furthermore, "it is the blood that makes atonement for the soul." Shed blood was necessary in both the Old and New Testaments to atone our souls with God. It is still a necessary requirement today.

Would you perhaps consider giving your time and blood to the Red Cross soon? Others are counting on you to be that bit of blessing to them. What a wonderful contribution you would be making for someone else!

God bless you in your journey today. Remember: it's in the blood!

Length of Days and a Long Life

Proverbs 3:1-2: "My son, forget not my law; but let thine heart keep my commandments: For length of days, and long life, and peace, shall they add to thee."

Want to know the secret to living a longer life? This verse was designed for you. According to the writer of Proverbs, you should follow diligently the laws of God and allow the commandments of God to permeate your life. This refers to the Ten Commandments in specific. If we keep the commandments and love the law of God and follow it, then we are promised a longer life and peace.

The Word of God is our teacher and guide and a light to our paths. If we are faithful and true to that Word, then our paths will be made straight. When we rebel and go our own way, disaster could occur. We never want to find ourselves outside of the Will of God. His Word instructs us in the way of wisdom and leads us in the paths of righteousness. He fills our hearts with peace and joy when we follow and obey.

God's love and faithfulness will never fail. Therefore, it is significant that we have God's Word in our hearts and always obey them.

Someone may ask, "Then what if I break just one of the commandments? Will I be eternally damned?" I would simply lead you to the greatest of all commandments that Jesus gave in the Word: "Thou shalt love the Lord thy God with all of thy heart, and with all thy soul, and with all thy mind. This is the first and great commandment. And the second is like unto it, 'Thou shalt love thy neighbour as thyself.'" Matthew 22:37-39 (KJV)

Furthermore, Jesus tells us in verse 40, "On these two commandments hang all the law and the prophets."

There you have it. If we are faithful and love God with all our hearts, souls, and minds, and love our neighbors as we love ourselves, then we shall live long and fruitful lives. If we do this, then we will not have time or the desire to do harm to anyone else! This IS the greatest and first commandment of all.

It is my heartfelt prayer that you will meditate on these things today and grow greatly in your faith. Resolve in your heart to follow this greatest commandment, and all the others will fall into order.

GOD, help my brother or sister today who may be struggling to find their way. May they reach out to you and give their all to you and your love for them. Receive them as your own and lead them in the paths of righteousness I pray.

God bless you on your journey today.

Bare Necessities

Matthew 6:25-34

In this passage, Jesus tells his followers not to be concerned about their lives and what they were to eat or drink, or even their clothing. Keep the main thing the main thing in life, and the main thing is Jesus!

In Matthew 6:21 we read, "For where your treasure is, there will your heart be also." (KJV) The treasure we seek is from the Word of God that always sheds light into the darkness of our lives. If we invest our lives in Christ, then our hearts will also reside with him.

The bare necessities of our lives are food, water, and shelter, without which we could not survive. We must have these things available to us if we are to prosper and follow God.

The bare necessities in a marriage are love, sharing, and caring for each other in any situation. I know an older couple who have been married now for 67 years! That is truly remarkable in our society today where over 50% of marriages end in divorce. When I asked them how they had managed to stay together for so long, the wife replied, "Because we have always loved each other and have respected each other. We never go to bed mad." What a wonderful testimony and example of love!

I love Matthew 7:7: 'Ask, and it shall be given you; seek, and ye shall find; knock, and it shall be opened unto you." (KJV) Isn't this one of the most beautiful passages of the Bible? It is so succinct and straightforward. If you want something from Christ, then ask for it. If you are looking for something, look for it. If you knock at the door, Jesus will open it to you.

I grew up with a painting of Jesus standing at someone's door. He is knocking at the door. I remember noticing that the painting did not have a doorknob on the outside, so Jesus could not enter without the person inside opening the door first. He is always standing at the door of our hearts knocking, but it is solely up to us to turn the knob and allow him entrance.

Finally, Matthew 6:33 sums it up for us: "But seek ye first the kingdom of God, and his righteousness; and all these things shall be added unto you."

There's the answer we've been searching for. If we put God first in our lives, then our bare necessities will be taken care of. He will provide our needs without hesitation.

In closing, let me quote another passage in Matthew 7:13-14: "Enter ye in at the strait gate: for wide is the gate, and broad is the way, that leadeth to destruction, and many there be which go in thereat; because strait is the gate, and narrow is the way, which leadeth unto life, and few there be that find it."

Coming to Christ involves entering through that narrow gate and, once inside, we find sustenance for our lives. Our bare necessities are taken care of if we trust in Him and obey His Word.

God bless you on your journey today.

Rejoice in the Lord Always!

Habakkuk: 3:18: "Yet I will rejoice in the Lord; I will take joy in the God of my salvation."

Philippians 4:4: "Rejoice in the Lord always: and again I say, Rejoice."

Years ago, I had a church member who had to spend two hours each Sunday morning emptying his colostomy and iliostomy bags and thoroughly cleansing himself to get ready for church. He always sat on the very front pew with a big smile on his face and thankful to just be alive! He came to the altar each time we had an altar call, and was always faithful to God and the church, and his prayer was often for other people. I wondered how in the world could he go through that arduous task and still make it to church when I have had others who woke up with a headache and decided to just stay in bed. And then I discovered his reason. He shared with me one day that he had met other people at the hospital where he had the two surgeries, and they were in worst condition than he was. He said that he had learned to be thankful in even the smallest of blessings!

The Apostle Paul learned to find joy while in prison. If he could do that, then so can we. I guess it all depends on your mindset. Even in the midst of terrible circumstances, people have found something to rejoice about, so, why can't we?

If we learn to focus on the positive aspects of our faith, we can find joy. We need to develop a positive spirit of gratitude for what we have, even though it may be hanging by a thread! Perhaps that's the reason for the scripture above that calls on each of us to "Rejoice in the Lord always." We need an attitude of gratitude if we are to truly live for Christ.

Many of you are perhaps going through troubling times today; so did Christ. Many of you have pain and suffering from debilitating diseases or illnesses; so did Christ. Many are being persecuted today; so was Christ. Stop playing the poor, poor pitiful me game and learn to be thankful in every situation. When we do that, we discover more and more of the grace and mercy of our Lord, as did my church member so many years ago. He fought a good fight and kept the faith, but he finally succumbed to his cancer a few years after I moved from that appointment. To this day, his example has been a major part of my inspiration and hope.

"Two men looked through prison bars; one saw mud, the other saw stars!" (Dale Carnegie)

It is all a matter of learning to praise the Lord in all things. What are you facing today that the Lord cannot handle? He will be there for you if you call upon Him. Be faithful and put your faith in His abilities. Give Him praise and He will bless you.

God bless you on your journey today.

Take Up Your Cross

Mark 8:34b: "Whosoever will come after me, let him deny himself, and take up his cross, and follow me."

I have preached numerous sermons on this verse of scripture over the years. It is divided into three parts for the perfect three-point-sermon.

First, if we are to follow Christ, we must learn to deny ourselves and put Christ first in everything. That's so hard for a person to do, for we like to be in complete control. However, if we are to be faithful to Him, we must set aside our desires for doing our own thing, and granting Christ the reins of our lives. God doesn't want just a part of us, but our entire being!

Secondly, we must "take up his cross." Do you have any idea what this means? It is actually a metaphor that speaks of our service of sacrifice and surrender to Him. Once we have accepted Him as our Lord and Savior, we must then be willing to surrender ourselves to His will and be ready to offer ourselves as a sacrifice to His kingdom here on earth.

Thirdly, we should "follow" Christ, regardless as to those who will reject us, laugh about us, and ridicule our standing in Him. Their opinions do not matter in the grand scheme of things.

Mark 8:36 reminds us: "For what shall it profit a man if he shall gain the whole world, and lose his own soul?" Following Christ is a requirement in living for Him.

If we are ashamed of Christ, then He will be ashamed of us. If we seek to follow Him, He will always be there for us.

I have seen a couple of men carrying a life-sized cross through the streets of town before, and perhaps you have as well. They have taken the scripture literally, but we do not have to do that. The cause of Christ in this world is more than enough for us to get busy and help bring about His kingdom to others. In doing so, we ARE carrying our cross to the world.

Lord, help us to deny ourselves, take up our own personal crosses, and follow you for the rest of our earthly lives. AMEN.

God bless you on your journey today.

To Lose Your Child

Luke 2:42-52

I trust that you will read the discourse above in your Bible. It would take up this entire page to reprint, so I am trusting you to read it as we discuss this passage.

It is set around the boy, Jesus, having reached the age of accountability in the Jewish faith. His family, Mary and Joseph, takes him to Jerusalem with them, which was an annual trip they made for the feast of Passover. At the end of the period, Mary and Joseph, along with the rest of their family and friends, left on foot and donkey to return home. This was an entire day's journey.

Before they reached home, they began to realize that Jesus wasn't with them. They immediately headed back to Jerusalem, looking all along the way for their precious son. In perhaps a panic mode, they searched everywhere for him, but he wasn't to be found. They knocked on every door and made constant inquiries about the boy. No luck! They had lost their son, the one given them by the Holy Spirit.

In desperation, after a three day search, they went to the temple where the celebration had taken place. There, they found their son, sitting among the doctors and leaders of the temple. He was listening to and absorbing everything they had to say. He asked them questions and answered many, and those gathered were amazed at the young boy for having such wisdom.

When Mary and Joseph found him, Mary grabbed him perhaps by the arms (as mother's often do) and asked him why he had remained behind. "Thy father and I have sought thee sorrowing." (verse 48b) And then Jesus dropped the bomb on them: "How is it that ye sought me? Wist ye not that I must be about my Father's business?" (verse 49)

Mary and Joseph had no idea what the child, Jesus, had just shared with them. So, they departed Jerusalem for the full day's journey back to Nazareth, their hometown, while pondering those thoughts in their minds.

We must not forget that this was God's very own Son and a gift from Heaven. He was sent through Mary and Joseph to be a sacrifice and blessing to the world. Perhaps they had forgotten? Had the first twelve years deadened their sensitivity to the calling upon their Son's life?

Verse 52 says: 'And Jesus increased in wisdom and stature, and in favour with God and man." He was now ready to begin taking on the responsibilities of God, as we should. We are to be about His business and the things which pertain to God.

God bless you on your journey today.

The Calling

Luke 4:18-19: "The Spirit of the Lord is upon me, because he hath anointed me to preach the gospel to the poor; he hath sent me to heal the brokenhearted, to preach deliverance to the captives, and recovering of sight to the blind, to set at liberty them that are bruised, To preach the acceptable year of the Lord."

The Spirit of the Lord laid a hand on my shoulder when I was seventeen, confirming my confession and acceptance that He was now Lord of my life. I did not know what was in store for me up the road, but I had been chosen for service of some kind. It would be a few years later when I felt the nudge again and the call upon my life while teaching a bible study in a large complex in Atlanta. God's Spirit witnessed with my spirit, and I knew I was ready. So, I returned home and started preparations for the ministry by taking my License to Preach study course. I wasn't quite sure that was what I would end up doing, but I was making progress.

Since then, I have preached for 54 years across South Georgia, witnessed in prisons and nursing homes, prayed with the sick and dying, commiserated and prayed with drug addicts and street people, and have married couples and buried the dead. At 72, I am still going strong. There are still so many things I hope to accomplish for the kingdom. Where, you may ask, do I get the impetus for doing these things? My answer is the Holy Spirit. Without Him to guide me, strengthen me, and encourage me, I would not be able to do all of these things. He is my hope and guide.

The requirements are simply stated in our scripture above, and I would challenge each of you to look for ways in which you could serve the Lord. A few examples are given in our scripture: preach or teach the gospel to the poor, heal the brokenhearted, preach deliverance and salvation to the imprisoned in jail and in their own mind, give vision to those who will not or cannot see, and give freedom to those who have been beaten and broken down by life. Whew! That's a lot for one person to do, but we are called to do just that. Therefore, there is no time to waste.

Think of the many creative ways that we can help people. You can learn how to teach a Sunday School class, share a witness in church on Sunday, minister to those living in low- rent housing, talk to a friend who may be down and out, go to the jail and ask if you could visit with one or two of those incarcerated and share your faith with them. There are people out there just crying for God to send someone to them. Be the change in their lives today.

God bless you on your journey today.

BE CHARITABLE

> I Corinthians 13:1, 14:1: "Though I speak with the tongues of men and of angels, and have not charity, I am become as sounding brass, or a tinkling cymbal. Follow after charity, and desire spiritual gifts."

Charity, or as many have refers to it as love, reflects how devoted and obedient we are to God. I could speak volumes to men and angels, but without charity, I am a loud horn or tinkling cymbal. When these two instruments are played alone, they make excruciating sounds! But when they are played in a band or orchestra, they blend in to the overall sound and purpose.

Charity is a reflection of God's love for humanity. Within the New Testament, I counted 28 times that Charity is mentioned as one of the supreme responsibilities of a Christian believer. Charity is generosity, kindness, and love toward others.

There are two things required in Paul's message to the church at Corinth: "Follow after charity, and desire spiritual gifts." When we love others, we usually receive love in return. When we do things for others, things are done for us.

My dear friend was shopping the other day at Sam's Club and noticed some really nice winter boots that were on sale, so, she bought both my wife and I a pair of them. That's charity. When we go out of way to help others in need, that's charity. When we practice generosity, kindness, and love, it always come back to us as a blessing.

The second part of Paul's message to the church was that we should "desire spiritual gifts." These are listed below and are from I Corinthians 12:4-11:

Word of wisdom, Word of knowledge, Faith, Gifts of healing, Working of miracles, Prophecy, Distinguishing between spirits, speaking in tongues, and interpreting tongues. These are all powerful gifts that the Holy Spirit bestows upon us when we are called to serve Him. These are just as important as charity. Both together makes for a well-rounded believer.

May you be blessed with an outpouring of God's spiritual gifts today.

God bless you on your journey today.

The Wages of Sin

Romans 6:23: "For the wages of sin is death; but the gift of God is eternal life through Jesus Christ our Lord."

My father found me smoking one day with a friend behind the barn. He took me aside, sent my friend home, and wore my pants nearly off my body with a switch he cut from our peach tree in the back yard. Furthermore, he told me that I could not see my friend, a nearby neighbor, for two weeks! He was my best playmate. Yet, I understood his scolding, took my punishment, and served the sentence. I always referred to it as a "little sin" back then, but there really aren't any little sins! They are sins, no matter how big or small.

Some people delight in the fact that any sins they have committed aren't nearly as egregious as those of others. For instance, someone commits murder or someone breaks a traffic law. Some would say that the murderer should suffer death for that sin, but the person breaking a simple law should go free. Do you see where I'm going with this? God doesn't weigh the severity of the sin, just the fact that we have sinned.

In James 1:14-15 we read: "But every man is tempted, when he is drawn away of his own lust, and enticed. Then when lust hath conceived, it bringeth forth sin: and sin, when it is finished, bringeth forth death." Yielding to temptation is our first sin; knowing that it will lead to something even worse and eventually to sin. Once we lust after something which is not ours, or something we know is wrong, then it becomes sin. James tells us that eventually it leads to our death.

Romans 3:9-10 reads: "What then? Are we better than they? No, in no wise: for we have before proved both Jews and Gentiles, that they are all under sin; As it is written, There is none righteous, no, not one."

In Christianity, we refer to the "Seven Deadly Sins." They are: Pride, Greed, Wrath, Lust, Envy, Gluttony and Sloth.

In addition to these, we commanded to follow and obey THE TEN COMMANDMENTS. We are surrounded then by laws and warnings about sinfulness and the direct result is always death. Study these and steer clear of anything that will cause you to stumble against the Lord and His holy statues. Keep a clear conscience and walk the straight path to salvation.

God bless you on your journey today.

How to Gain Your Life

> Matthew 16:25-26: "For whosoever shall save his life will lose it: and whosoever shall lose his life for my sake shall find it. For what is a man profited, if he shall gain the whole world, and lose his own soul? Or what shall a man give in exchange for his soul?"

Priorities! We all have them. They should dictate to us the way we live our lives. If we believe in God, then our priorities should align with His.

I decided fifty-two years ago to ask my wife if she would marry me. She said, "Yes!" and I've made her one of my top priorities through the years. Of course, I grow weary of the honey do lists, but I try to maintain the harmony between us because I love her. And then, the two of us became four. Our son and daughter became our priorities. We both agreed to have each of them and have invested our time, money, and energies into their raising. Our son became the valedictorian of his graduating class and an engineer. Our daughter graduated with a teacher's degree, and she teaches Kindergarten today. We could not be prouder of them.

And then, two little grandchildren came along! Again, we have invested our time, money and energies into seeing that their needs are met.

Fifty-five years ago, I invited Jesus to come into my life and create a new creature. He did, and from that day forward, I have made him my number-one priority! My wife knows that he comes first! My children and grandchildren also know. I have dedicated my life since then to full-time ministry in the church and missions. When we seek to follow Christ in all things, then everything else just falls into place.

Our scripture talks about prioritizing our faith over worldly things. We all seem to follow what is most important to us. You can usually measure the faith of a Christian by their walk and talk, and where they seem to place their priorities. Where are your priorities today? Have you talked to God about them? Do we place too much emphasis on earthly possessions instead of the things of God? Perhaps we need to think today about what is truly important to us, and how we can align our actions to our values. Is God your number-one priority? If not, then why not? We only find ourselves in Christ when he is our top priority; second place will not do!

We all must make sacrifices to stay true to Christ. Sometimes, I'm afraid, we are reluctant to make those sacrifices, and our spiritual life suffers greatly. What things are you willing to give in exchange for your soul? In all depends on your level of faith and how willing you are to put God first. When we seek him with our whole hearts, we will find him at the point of our greatest need.

God bless you on your journey today.

"Whom Shall I Send?"

Isaiah 6:8: "And I heard the voice of the Lord, saying, Whom shall I send, and who will go for us? Then said I, Here am I; send me."

When I accepted Christ as my Lord and Savior, I was at rock-bottom with no way up! I knew that my life was a mess when a friend told me about Jesus. I was not a Bible reader but knew about the Bible from attending church occasionally with my mother. So, my friend invited me one night to a Campus Crusade for Christ rally, and I felt my heart warmed that evening to the prospects of salvation. While praying with my friend, I felt the movement of the Holy Spirit upon me and began crying unmercifully. I then prayed for that same Spirit to come into my heart, and He did! I said yes to God that night and have been serving Him since. I heard God calling that night, and I answered.

This passage of scripture reveals a vision Isaiah had earlier in the temple that described the holiness of God and how unworthy Isaiah was amid that holiness. In a similar fashion, we are all unworthy of God, but He makes a way for us to receive His grace and mercy through the blood of Jesus. His death on the cross and the shedding of His innocent blood cover our sins when we receive Him in faith, believing in His ability to transform us and heal our sinfulness. We need to recognize our own sinfulness before we can align ourselves with God. We must be willing to leave the old and partake of the new if we are to answer His call upon our lives.

Before his calling, an angel (verses 6 and 7) symbolically cleanses Isaiah from his sins and prepares him to accept God's invitation. At that moment of cleansing, Isaiah hears God's voice calling him to preach to the nation of Israel, calling them to repentance. Isaiah's exuberance then became apparent as he would begin a life of total dedication to God and the preaching of God to the nation.

It is essential for us to fall under the conviction that we are sinners before we accept the goodness and grace of the Almighty. Once we are convinced that we are sinners, in need of salvation, we then experience the calling upon our lives.

The first day after my salvation experience, I found a skinny little black tie and wore it to school with the only white shirt I had. I felt like I needed to look the part of a changed person to others. When I got to school, my best friend told me that I did not have to do that to show others I had changed. He told me that change takes place in the heart, not outwardly.

God bless you on your journey today.

Trust in the Lord

Proverbs 3:5-6: "Trust in the Lord with all thine heart; and lean not unto thine own understanding. In all thy ways acknowledge him, and he shall direct thy paths."

Romans 8:28 says: "All things work together for the good of those who trust God."

We are never promised an absolutely good or easy life here on earth. We will have troubles and trials and will be persecuted at times, but the promise of God is that He will make a way for us. Our troubles and trials serve only to make us stronger. The child of God never trusts trust in his/her own understanding, but trusts in the wisdom and knowledge received from the word of God.

Job is one of our greatest examples. He has often been referred to as "the suffering servant." While facing the loss of everything in his life - children, farm, animals, home, his wife - he is faced with nothing left but himself. Yet, Job still does not relent from his faith in God. He stands firm, knowing that God has never let him down before and would never desert him. It is when we trust God with our entire being that our faith becomes the strongest. My understanding of this life is so very little that I dare not trust in my understanding of it to survive! I have made some terrible mistakes and it was because of my lack of faith in the One who could see me through. After I accepted his love, mercy, and grace, everything began to fall into place in my life.

I recall Job's friends all tried to convince him to deny his god, but Job stood firm in his faith, unwavering. And you can too. May your belief in the risen Lord give you strength and comfort today in the midst of your stormy seas.

God bless you on your journey today.

Rejoice, Pray, and Give Thanks

I just preached a sermon yesterday on I Thessalonians Chapter Five, where the apostle Paul gives three imperatives for living the Christian life. We should rejoice always, pray without ceasing, and give thanks in every situation. These are tough sounding imperatives, but they are necessary if we want to live the God-chosen lifestyle He has called us to live. Let us take them one at a time and see how they affect our daily lives.

#1 - REJOICE ALWAYS.

When things are running smoothly in our lives we tend to rejoice. But what happens when we are confronted with inconvenient situations or almost insurmountable odds? Do we flinch and take the "poor, poor is me!" attitude? Do we run, hide, and hope that the tough situation soon goes away? No! Paul tells us that, because of God's goodness, faithfulness, and grace, we should not have a change in attitude when these situations occur. We should remain steadfast and learn to REJOICE in every situation or circumstance.

I know all too well that people have difficulty with this stance in life, and rightfully so. If our faith is not strong and courageous, then we will balk at anything that does not make us happy. We only want good things to come our way. Did we not sign up for night fishing in a small boat on the Sea of Galilee, with a bunch of other disciples, when a storm arises and threatens to topple us over? Did we not sign up for that angry co-worker who looks to destroy our job by lying to the boss about something we really have not done? There are all sorts of conditions we find ourselves in each day that we should be capable of handling with a spirit of learning to rejoice in every situation. It takes practice and a whole lot of faith, but we should learn to always be faithful, no matter what.

Times are tough out there today and we need a few night fishermen with an unwavering faith when the storms of life come. I gladly welcome such tests to try my spirit and to bolster my faith, and so should you. Just remember, when they do come (and they will!) be prepared and ready to rejoice in that situation. God will bless your obedience and faith.

#2 - PRAY WITHOUT CEASING.

I was lying on a gurney, a few weeks ago, on my way down the hall to the operating room. I began to pray that God would take charge of my surgery, the attendants, and the surgeon. I did not close my eyes in the process, but prayed, nonetheless. My life, at that point, became a life of prayer, accepting God's Will in my surgery and the outcome.

The other day, prior to my surgery, I sat in the doctor's office noticing a man across the room from me who was in excruciating pain. He was poorly dressed and seemed to be having a rough day of things. I found myself praying for him and asking God to pour out a blessing upon him. It is the little prayers like that which Paul encourages us to do all day, every day. We should PRAY WITHOUT CEASING!

Talking to God throughout the day becomes a Christian point-of-view and living. We are always on the lookout for those whom we think need a good prayer. Be a prayer-warrior and bring hope to someone's life today and God will bless you in return.

Also, we should constantly ask God for guidance and wisdom to discern such situations we confront. I have found myself looking at life through an entirely different Lense when I practice praying without ceasing. God reveals more of himself to us when we are constantly praying, and it reminds us of God's presence within us. When this occurs, we experience His comfort.

#3 - GIVE THANKS IN ALL CIRCUMSTANCES.

You must be kidding me, preacher! How can we give thanks in every single circumstance? Sometimes I get mad and want to lash-out at people! Sometimes I want to let other people know exactly how mad I am with them! No, no, no! We should never do those things. We are representatives of the risen Lord and should imitate Him and what He would do in such circumstances. The key is for us to find hope amid despair. It is there; we just have to look for it. God has already provided for us all that is necessary in our lives. He protects us and loves us through any situation. That should give us confidence to face the many trials we will meet along life's way.

All three of these Christian imperatives will prove to affect your lives if you will practice them daily. Others will also receive blessings from God as an indirect result of your prayers, thanksgivings, and praise.

Remember Paul and Silas behind bars in a dirty, dingy, filthy prison? (Acts 16:16-34) They could have simply given up and called it quits, but their faith was too strong to allow them to pity their situation. They both rose to the occasion and began praying with ceasing, singing and rejoicing over their atrocious surroundings, and giving thanks that, even in prison, God was with them! Soon, the prison doors were opened by an earthquake that shook the prison, and God freed them from their shackles. He will do the same for each of you if you will only remain faithful. In doing so, you will experience inner peace and joy like you have never known before. What a mighty God we serve!

God bless you on your journey today.

Living the Cleansed Life

> II Kings 5:14: "Then went he (Naaman) down, and dipped himself seven times in Jordan, according to the saying of the man of God: and his flesh came again like unto the flesh of a little child, and he was clean."

This is a beautiful story of a cleansed life. Naaman was a captain of the king of Syria's fleet. He was strong and determined to do his master's will. He would actually give his life to protect the life of his king, as would most loyal soldiers.

But Naaman had one big problem: he was a leper. A leper was someone who had developed large boils on his body, and most people thought the leprosy was contagious. Even in the days of Jesus, lepers were found to be unclean and, thus, were excommunicated from their homes and villages, most of them finding homes in the caves and crevices of the mountains. It was a life of shame, although it wasn't their fault. Leprosy was a disease then without a cure, so people would keep their distance from an infected person. Life, as a leper, was usually lived among other lepers where they could commiserate with one another. It had to have been a tragic life at the least.

There was a servant girl who came to work with Naaman's wife as a maid, who saw the beginnings of Naaman's leprosy and suggested that he go and visit the old prophet in Samaria who could help him recover from the leprosy. The king of Syria agreed that Naaman should go and present himself to the prophet for healing. The king of Israel was angry when he read the letter from the Syrian king. "Who does he think I am? GOD? I do not have the power to do such."

When Elisha heard about Naaman's situation, he invited him to come to his house. He sent a messenger out to Naaman and told him to go and dip seven times in the river of Jordan and it would cleanse him. Naaman thought it was a hoax and would not agree to such a dumb solution. He went away in a rage of unbelief. And then his men came unto him begging him to listen to the prophet and do as he told him. Naaman reluctantly went to the river Jordan and dipped the required seven times and, behold, he came up the seventh time cleansed!

Was it the first dip in the river that did the trick? No! It was only after the required seventh dip that he was healed! There was really nothing magical about the seventh time, but truly a testing of Naaman's faith. If he would follow the prophet's instructions, then he would be healed.

God requires his children to trust and obey, no matter how ridiculous the requests may seem. It is the faith we put into action from God's word that brings us the victory we seek. Trust him today in order to live the cleansed life.

God bless you on your journey today.

What Can You Offer the Lord?

Judges 3:31: "And after him was Shamgar the son of Anath, which slew of the Philistines six hundred men with an ox goad: and he also delivered Israel."

Some years ago, I took an old hymn entitled, "And They Were Used of God" and wrote my own version from it. The writer of the words was "anonymous," and the writer of the music was A. P. Main.

"Shamgar had an ox cart, Moses had a rod.

Little David had a slingshot, and they were used by God." (Charles Cravey version)

Shamgar simply had an ox cart that he was asked to take into battle against the mighty Philistines. He only had an ox goad with him that he used in driving his team of oxen from place to place. There were no rifles or guns to subdue the Philistines in that day and most commentaries say that the "goad" was a large stick. It is somewhat ludicrous to even think that he was responsible for slaying six hundred men with a large stick! The commentaries all tend to think that Shamgar was the leader of the Israelite army that went up against the Philistines. He did, however, lead them with a stick! God had blessed it and sent he and his army out against the Philistine army and defeated them.

Moses had the rod which God had blessed and given to him from the burning bush story. He used that rod to part the Red Sea when the Israelites were escaping the Egyptians. That rod became a symbol of God's presence and miraculous works from that day forward.

Little shepherd, David, went up against the mighty Goliath in battle with only a slingshot and a stone and defeated him! Again, God takes what we have, blesses it, and uses it for his kingdom. Those elements that we think are small and inconsequential, become mighty in the hands of those blessed of God.

What do you have in your hands? A slingshot, a goad, or a rod? Perhaps it is wisdom, faith, devotion, and determination. Whatever you have God can bless it and use it to build his great kingdom here on earth.

It wasn't until after my first mission trip to Costa Rica, that I realized that my ministry could do wonderful things in a different setting. I remember once that 36 young people came to accept the Lord as Savior during a vacation bible school that our team held in Guyana,

Central America. We were common folk from South Georgia and had only the desire and love for other people; yet, we were able to teach from God's word enough for those 36 youth to come to Christ!

God bless you on your journey today. What do you have that God can use?

Creating Something from Nothing

> Genesis 1:27: "So God created man in his own image, in the image of God created he him."

My wife, Renee, will gather all her materials for her work and escape to one of our back bedrooms. There, she will meticulously sketch her intended work on a canvas until she has it exactly right. Now, for the next four or five hours, undisturbed, she will take brush in hand and begin the creation of something beautiful and lasting from what once was a blank slate! Artists have been doing this throughout the centuries. The "great" ones have paintings hanging in some of the greatest art galleries in the world. Others, like Renee, hang theirs on living room walls or the walls of their friends. Hers is not for sale. She gives them away, although they are good enough to sell in the market. The work and time she invests into each painting cannot be measured in monetary funds. She does the work willingly for pure satisfaction. It thrills her that a friend wants a certain painting to hang on their wall!

Renee creates something from nothing. What was once a blank canvas becomes a beautiful landscape that peaks one's imagination. We have her paintings on every wall in our home, and the others (that have not been given away) are stacked in one of our bedroom closets. One day, she will give her paintings to someone visiting us who takes an interest in her work.

Creating something from nothing is also the work of our Lord. He takes the dust of the earth, molds it in his hands with a little spittle and mud, and creates man and woman. He takes a wayward child and leads him in the paths of righteousness, and the child becomes a great man of God.

Renee has a scene in mind before she commits it to the canvas. She knows where she is going with the painting, although the canvas is blank.

I write and record music. I am not a maestro at it, but I have had success in the field of gospel music for years. When I write a song, I begin with a melody in my head, pick up my guitar, or sit at the piano, and the words begin coming. It contributes to my love of God, and it is one way I have found to give him praise, glory, and honor. When the work is completed, I listen to it and know that God was the creator of the song, not me.

The great composers of the past created beautiful music and songs that we appreciate today. Some of those songs or musical scores took several years to create. You and I do not see the struggle and work of the composer, but we can hear the beauty of the finished product.

The renowned artist Michelangelo was commissioned to paint frescoes on the ceiling of the Sistine Chapel in Rome in the early 1500s. It is the place where bishops and popes have been commissioned for their roles in the church. Over the course of four years, Michelangelo stood endlessly on scaffolding for hours each day to paint the twelve disciples and several prophets. It is a remarkable masterpiece of art and a treasure to the Vatican and those who see it. We are moved by its beauty and the untiring work of the master artist!

What will you create today? The other night, I was listening to a motivational speaker who suggested that we should have one thing we wish to accomplish each day when we awake from sleep. There may be many other things during the day we hope to accomplish, but that one thing we decide upon should be our priority. Why not prioritize that one thing today and begin tomorrow? He also said that, to increase our knowledge and memory, we should read one book per week! Wow! Who does that? Maybe if we set our goal at one book per month we would be more successful. The key for us is to START.

What will you create today? God bless you on your journey.

Just One Rose Will Do

My mother loved flowers. Our yard was covered with them. As a child, my job was helping her dig up weeds that would try to encroach upon those flowers. From those early days, I gained a deep appreciation for their beauty and the work that went into their growth. She would teach me certain aspects of each plant and how to care for them. One of her favorite plants was the rose. We had various species of plants growing throughout the spring and summer months, but her rose gardens were the spectator's favorites. They came in pink, red, yellow, orange, and a few other colors I can't describe.

Mama always said that whenever she died, she did not want flowers at her funeral. A favorite old hymn of hers was, "Just One Rose Will Do", and that was her request - One Rose!

My mother had worked with the local funeral home years before she died to make plans for her funeral. She paid on it each month to have it paid off when she passed. She did not want the children to worry about burial fees, so she took care of that important matter for us in advance. Mama was that way, very frugal, and she made every penny count. She paid for an old, dilapidated house that I grew up in for years by saving her extra money and paying the mortgage as much as she could each month.

When mama passed, my family sold her home and divided the proceeds among ourselves - a gift from mama! A few days after the house had sold, Renee and I went to the house and found one of her rose bushes. We immediately dug it up and brought it home to plant in our yard. That was fifteen years ago, and that bush, although spindly and small, still produces only one rose each season. We have put fertilizer and rose food around it each year, yet it still produces only one lone rose! Is this mama's way of reminding us of what's important in life? She did not make a fuss over what other people had but spent her life trying hard to supply her family's needs. And she did it well.

I have seen a lot of roses in the years since, but none are as beautiful as mama's little rose. It is a deep red and always reminds me of her. At the present, her memory continues to live on as I await that rose each season. I watch the bud become a flower, much like my life. Mama provided what I needed growing up and taught me what was important in this life - the love and care of a family. She never wanted anyone to fuss over her. Just keep it simple.

Perhaps today, we should take care of the important things in our lives.

God bless you on your journey today.

The Potter and the Clay

Isaiah 64:8: "O Lord, thou art our father; we are the clay, and thou art our potter; and we are the work of thy hand."

The scripture above says it all. God is our creator and we are part of his creation. He fashioned us with his own hands and created the best possible creature.

I have been in a potter's shop before in the mountains of North Carolina. I stood there for a couple of hours looking at him take a block of clay, slapping it on the potter's wheel, wetting his hands, and beginning the arduous task of forming that mound into a beautiful pot. He would whistle as he worked like he really enjoyed the artistry he was performing. I would occasionally comment on how awesome he was at bringing the pot into existence. He said, "It's all right there in that mound of clay. There's either a pot, bowl, or container of some kind already in there. I just have to bring it out!"

In the same way, God has taken the mound of earth and created something beautiful of our lives. The master's touch has transformed us into that which he would have us be. The rest is up to us. We must decide how we will live our lives. Will we dedicate them to good or to evil?

When he had finished, he took the well-designed pot and placed it in his kiln where it would be "fired" through the rest of that day and night. The firing cures the clay by hardening it. He showed me finished pots and they were spectacular. He truly was a master at his craft and I was greatly impressed at his work.

He then invited me to take a block of clay, sit at the wheel, and try to make something out of it. I messed it up completely! I tried twice again, but to no avail. I could not get it to work for me. There is a skill that I am not good at. In fact, I flunked the test and decided then and there that I was not a potter. I'll just stick to my music and ministry.

In the grand scheme of things, we have been created to serve God. He has set the stage for us to follow his holy will. It is when we are mislead or taking astray by our own desires and weaknesses, that we wind up on the potter's floor; broken shards that are worthless. But then the master takes to the clay again and fashions us into that which we were created to be. That, to me, is salvation; although undeserved.

God bless you on your journey today.

Saddest Truth in Scripture

To me, the saddest truth in all of scripture is not the fact that there is going to be many bad people in hell, but rather the fact that there is going to be many good people in hell.

Some years ago, a church member invited me to use his deer stand at the edge of the woods on his property. He loaned me one of his guns and handed me a box of shells, and told me to get to the stand before daybreak. I was excited, since this was my first time hunting deer, so I loaded everything into the truck the following morning and drove out to the area where he told me to park. I then walked about a quarter of a mile to the deer stand as quietly as possible, and climbed into the stand. About a half hour later, while I was freezing to death in that stand, I heard a loud snort in the distance. Out of the midst walked this huge Buck deer and came within 20 feet of me. I slowly picked up the rifle and pointed it at the deer and pulled the trigger when he was in sight. Click goes the gun and off bounded that big buck. Of all things, I forgot to load the gun! I really felt like a stupid heel at that point, so I got down from the stand and walked back to my truck. I decided from that day on that I would not deer hunt ever again.

There are going to be many good people who do not make it to heaven because, if you will, they were not fully prepared or ready. They may have been to church regularly throughout their lives; they may have taught a Sunday School class or filled in for the pastor. These people could have been the epitome of the "perfect" human being, but if their hearts were not in the right place, they are still lost.

Matthew 7:21-23: "Not every one that saith unto me, Lord, Lord, shall enter into the kingdom of heaven; but he that doeth the will of my Father which is in heaven. Many will say to me in that day, Lord, Lord, have we not prophesied in thy name? And in thy name have cast out devils? And in thy name done many wonderful works? And then I will profess unto them, I never knew you: depart from me, ye that work iniquity."

What a discourse for those who would seek easy entry into heaven. Just because we have done wonderful things for the kingdom does not give us entry. The scripture is clear about these people. They have cast out demons from others, prophesied in the Lord's name, yet, they are still lost!

So, how do we make it to heaven? We are saved by trusting Christ as our personal Lord and Savior, accepting his salvation, and giving our lives completely to him. God's salvation is free. The acknowledgment of our sins is the first step towards God, confessing those sins to the Savior, and turning from a life of sin to follow Jesus.

Why are so many of us miserable today? Because we have never obeyed God completely. We have failed to do what the word of God teaches us to do.

Luke 10:27: "Thou shalt love the Lord thy God with all thy heart, and with all thy soul, and with all thy strength, and with all thy mind; and thy neighbour as thyself."

This passage gives us the answer to living a saved life. Loving God and neighbor are the two greatest laws of Jesus. We do that with heart, soul, mind and strength.

Don't forget to load your gun!

God bless you on your journey today.

A Cure for What Ails You

Luke 24:36: "Peace be unto you."

Shalom! This is the Old Testament word for "peace." There is really nothing better you could wish for your family or friends. Peace is the absence of confusion and discord. It is positive and symbolizes our wholeness. We have harmony in our lives if we have this peace.

Paul says in Romans 15:13: "Now the God of hope fill you with all joy and peace to believing, that ye may abound in hope, through the power of the Holy Ghost." God is truly the source of our hope and peace and should be trusted to fulfill both in our lives. It is when we live outside of his holy will that we live in discord and confusion. The hope, joy and peace of God will cure whatever ails you.

One of the best ways to seek that cure is to surround ourselves with good Christian people. When we fellowship with like-minded people, we tend to grow in our faith and receive ways in which they have grown in theirs. Praying with them, worshiping with them, and sharing things in common will help us to move closer to the Lord.

We must also recognize God as the sovereign entity of our lives. He desires our complete being. Let him know that he is in control of our lives and we remain loyal to him. Remember the times when God has been faithful to you and the blessings he brought into your life. Such times will serve as reminders of his goodness and mercy.

Read his word, obey his commands and trust in his great promises. All of these things will lead us closer to the Savior. The cure for what ails us is as simple as our next prayer. Humble yourself before God and seek his holy will for your life. He will hear and respond to the need for your cure.

God bless you on your journey today.

A Monopoly on the Spirit

Acts 2:4: "And they were all filled with the Holy Ghost, and began to speak with other tongues, as the Spirit gave them utterance."

It is said that in a pastor's meeting, the subject came up about having an evangelistic revival in the city. One pastor suggested asking Dwight L. Moody to be the speaker each night, and most everyone agreed. One pastor, however, asked why Moody was their first choice. He asked if Moody had a monopoly on the Holy Spirit. "No," said one pastor, "but the Holy Spirit has a monopoly on Dr. Moody!"

It is vital to understand that the Holy Spirit works through the able and willing bodies of believers to bring about the works of God. Dwight L. Moody was no exception. He was one of the greatest preachers at the time, but he had been led solely by God's Spirit to accomplish greatness in the kingdom. We are only successful in spreading God's word when we are led by the Spirit.

On the day of Pentecost, Acts 2:1-13, we can see the mighty hand of God working among those who had gathered that day. Jesus had already told the disciples before his ascension into heaven to expect the Holy Spirit to come upon them not many days from then. When it came, it was like a rushing, mighty wind, like a burning, raging fire, like a movement they had never experienced before! Their lives would never again be the same. That is what the indwelling of the Holy Spirit does to someone. It changes their lives in so many ways. We begin to speak differently, walk differently, and live our lives differently. It is a transformation the likes of which we have never known.

Those who had gathered that day were filled to the brim with the Spirit and began to do miraculous things in the sight of hundreds of witnesses. They were even accused of being drunk! When the Holy Spirit enters a person, amazing events occur. Those nearby can become warm to its glow and transform because of what they see.

Does the Holy Spirit have a monopoly on your soul? If not, then why not? Why do you hesitate to experience the greatest moment of your life? God is calling you forth to receive this gift, but you must make the first move. He does not come into our lives without us inviting him. Be filled to the brim today and experience joy like you have never experienced before.

God bless you on your journey today.

A Clear Conscience

I believe that the road to happiness is for one to first have a clear conscience. Knowing that you have done nothing wrong is the greatest start to any day. Knowing that you have not hurt anyone else is a blessing. Knowing that your life is an example for others to follow is supreme.

Martin Luther, a German priest and theologian in the 1500s, once said in his book, A *Babylonian Captivity of the Church*, "From the beginning of my Reformation, I have asked God to send me neither dreams nor visions nor angels, but to give me the right understanding of His Word, the Holy Scriptures; for as long as I have God's Word, I know that I am walking in His way and that I shall not fall into any error or delusion." Luther's one desire was to give himself fully and completely to God and his word. In immersing ourselves in that same word, we allow God to work through us.

Benjamin Franklin called a clear conscience "the best tranquilizer." Having a clear conscience helps us fall asleep quicker and awaken more refreshed. It is like having a sleeping pill to enable our sleep. Our conscience becomes the proverbial pill that enables us to sleep well.

In John 8:9, we read: "And they which heard it, being convicted by their own conscience, went out one by one, and Jesus was left alone, and the woman standing in the midst." This passage follows the story of Jesus confronting an angry mob of men in the city street one day who were in the process of stoning a woman caught in the act of adultery. In verse seven, Jesus had already said to the men, "He that is without sin among you, let him first cast a stone at her." One could assume that some of the men in that crowd had slept with the woman in the past, but here, they were being hypocritical.

After hearing Jesus and watching him write in the sand with his finger, the men turned away from the woman, knowing their sins were just as egregious as the adulterer. A person with a clear conscience is never hypocritical. When we have one finger pointed at another person, remember that we have three fingers pointed back at ourselves!

Paul admonishes fellow Christians in I Corinthians 8:9: "And their conscience being weak is defiled." Again, in verse nine, he says, "But take heed lest by any means this liberty of yours become a stumbling block to them that are weak." A clear conscience does not give us the liberty of condemning others. When we do so we are weak, and our faith is defiled. We are to forgive and love each other as Jesus loved us.

In Acts 24:16, we read: "And herein do I exercise myself, to have always a conscience void of offence toward God, and toward men." We should always strive for a clear conscience, blameless and sinless and never offend God or man with a condescending nature.

Paul again shares the following in II Corinthians 1:12: "Our rejoicing is this, the testimony of our conscience, that in simplicity and godly sincerity, not with fleshly wisdom, but by the grace of God, we have had our conversation in the world, and more abundantly to youward." Our testimony before God and the world is one of clear conscience, simplicity, sincerity, and wisdom. Only God's grace enables us to follow his will and to obey his commands. We do not seek to condemn others for to do so would be the condemning of ourselves! Keep a pure heart, without being corrupted by the ways of the world. Stay true to the word of God. Love your friends AND your enemies. In doing so, you will have opened the door to ministry with the world.

God bless you on your journey today.

Consider the Lilies

My wife and I love daylilies. They have exceptionally large blossoms, and many of them have a sweet aroma. They highlight two beds in our yard and have attracted passersby for years. We love the Peace lilies, Canna lilies, Asian lilies, and Stargazers the most.

Some years ago, a dear friend invited us to her garden to dig up as many daylilies as we wanted. Her health was failing, and she could no longer care for them. So, Renee, my wife, and I went crazy and brought home at least forty or fifty to plant in our two beds. Dorma, our benefactor, passed a few years ago, but her lasting memory blooms each year in our yard! Her generosity lives on.

Matthew 6:28-29 says: "And why take ye thought for raiment? Consider the lilies of the field, how they grow; they toil not, neither do they spin: And yet I say unto you, that even Solomon in all his glory was not arrayed like one of these."

This passage is in the Sermon on the Mount that Jesus delivered to many gathered to hear him on this occasion. In this passage, Jesus stresses that if God is concerned about the lowly lilies of the field, so much more he cares for you and me. He emphasizes that the lilies are here today and gone tomorrow, but God's care is endless, so we should never concern ourselves with material needs. God supplies. It is our spiritual needs we should be most concerned about. Seeking God fully brings us a bountiful supply of his Spirit.

We are to be fruitful and blossom wherever we are. You have heard the saying, "Bloom where you are planted," I am sure. It sounds biblical but is not in the Bible. The sentiment is that regardless of our situation, we are to do the best that we can. When we are down look up to the Savior who will give the increase. He will not fail us nor forsake us.

Plant some lilies today and bring beauty into your life. God bless you on your journey today.

Speak Truth

With a former U. S. President spouting daily lies and misinformation in the media and the religious right calling him God's choice for President, we have lost our true north when it comes to the truth. Where, I wonder, can truth be found today? During this former president's first campaign, I remember the lady who helped lead his campaign and who first coined the phrase "alternative truth." This was a ploy to hoodwink the American public into believing their lies over what was actually true. The campaign also said that all news that was not in their favor was "fake news." Deep in the psyche of America, we know what the truth is. It is never "alternative" or "fake." The truth is found in the Word of God.

Zechariah 8:16-17 states: "These are the things that you should do; Speak ye every man the truth to his neighbour; execute the judgment of truth and peace in your gates: And let none of you imagine evil in your hearts against his neighbour; and love no false oath: for all these are things that I hate, saith the Lord."

If we are to maintain a society espousing truth, we have these commands before us:

- Speak truth to our neighbors.
- Execute the judgment of truth.
- Have peace among us and our neighbors.
- Do not imagine evil in your heart or against your neighbor.
- Love no false oath (plotting evil against your neighbor).

In Psalms 25:10, we read, "All the paths of the Lord are mercy and truth unto such as keep his covenant and his testimonies." Christians follow the truth, not politics. Christians follow Christ, not some candidate.

The paths to God are through mercy, truth, and those who keep God's covenant. Through our testimonies, we prove our Christianity. We do not rely on someone else to tell us what to believe when the Word of God is already clear.

I realize how long Christians have wanted to overturn Roe v. Wade. I realize that Christians have wanted America to turn back to the moral majority. But at what cost? Should we give up our very souls to pass a few laws which do not cover the majority? God forbid.

The first thing on a Christian's agenda should be to follow the truth. God's Word is implicit in that respect. We are to love justice, follow the law, love our neighbors, seek the truth in all matters, and give ourselves to the will of God. I do not see that among the religious right today. I see a group of frustrated Christians who have been caught-up in a terrible fraud by an evil and wicked movement. If we lose this battle for truth, we have only ourselves to blame. If we continue to believe in "alternative" or "fake" news, then we ARE the problem and we continue to support it with vigor. When is it time for us to return to our first love, Jesus Christ, and give homage to Him instead of false prophets?

John 8:32 states, "And ye shall know the truth, and the truth shall make you free." Victor Frankl was a Jewish/Austrian prisoner of war during World War II and survived the Holocaust. In his book, Man's Search for Meaning, Frankl describes how he kept his humanity against inhumane ways. His fellow Jewish prisoners were demeaned, mistreated, beaten, and made to work until they could work no longer. They truly had little to eat, and survival seemed impossible. Amid such desperation, Frankl found his faith in God strong enough to help him remain focused on the main thing. As he looked around daily at others in his barrack dying of disease, hunger, or rat bites, he knew that his demise was inevitable. Yet, Frankl remained faithful to God in every way. He prayed constantly that God would deliver he and his fellow prisoners, and the truth would eventually prevail.

Today, we know the truth. Amid Holocaust deniers, history remains true. Over six million Jews were annihilated or died of terrible causes in those prisoner of war camps. As you recall, this was because of one's man's warped idea that Jews were going to take over the world if he did not do something about it! One man, filled with hatred and animosity toward others, filled with revenge in his heart, changed the landscape of the world. Does this bring anyone else to mind?

"And ye shall know the truth, and the truth shall make you free." There is a lot of talk about a "Free America" today and a lot of flags raising. The last time I checked in with the truth, America IS free! Our American flag stands taller today than ever! One of the flags we should be waving is the Christian flag, but that is another article all together.

Know the truth, my friend, and you shall be free!

God bless you on your journey today.

Endurance in the Wilderness

For years, I have taught Boy Scouts how to endure extreme situations, how to read a compass and find the true North, and how to prepare well before going on a journey. They must be told what to expect and how to respond. The Boy Scout manual is the Bible to a scout, but few read it from cover to cover. Our motto is: BE PREPARED! How many of us read the Bible like a road map? You can, you know. The scriptures and examples of faith and endurance fill each page with heroes of our faith who endured some of the most extreme situations one could ever face.

Matthew 4 is a good example for us to follow. Following John's baptism of Jesus in the Jordan River, the Spirit leads Jesus into a wilderness area where Satan tempts him materially. If Jesus is to be the Savior of the world, then he must endure the temptations of that world. In three succinct temptations, we can see the character of Jesus shining through. Let us take them one by one to see how each may affect our faith and walk in Christ.

The first thing that happens in the wilderness is his fasting for forty days and nights. Who among us could do that? Could we survive without food and water for those days? It is highly unlikely, given our current lifestyles. We are accustomed to eating three square meals a day, which is abundant in most cases. To do without the sustenance it takes to keep us alive would be our death sentence! But with Jesus, he realized the importance of enduring through this period in his life to help others along life's way later.

So, first, Jesus endures fasting. It would be good for us to fast occasionally, for it serves many worthwhile purposes (i.e., it cleanses the body; it strengthens the mind; it helps us concentrate on the main things in life we may be facing). Hunger is a vital issue across the world. There are people in villages across Africa who do not have ample food supplies. We read about children, as well as adults, going hungry for weeks at a time before someone delivers supplies to them. What happens when those supplies never arrive? The people die.

The first temptation Jesus encounters in the wilderness deals with the issue of food. Satan, knowing that Jesus was now hungry following his fast, was tempted to turn stones into bread. This is what I refer to as a material need. We are often tempted to give-in to an easier way of doing things instead of enduring the life given to us. Many have chosen this route in life and are paying the consequences now for doing things the straightforward way. Our society today is a prime example of folks doing things that way, and our society is in shambles. We have become gluttonous, envious, and lazy. We allow others to do the necessary things for us to help simplify our lives. Yet, this is not the best way. Jesus rebukes Satan in verse 4: "It is written, Man shall not live by bread alone, but by every word that proceedeth out of the mouth of God." Bread is the effortless way out. Standing firm in our beliefs that God will provide if we follow his will and way becomes our motto in life. Look to Jesus, not Satan.

Secondly, there is the physical temptation of Jesus in the wilderness. Satan takes Jesus to the pinnacle of the temple and tempts him to jump off, knowing that it would certainly kill him. Jesus, realizing what Satan is attempting to get him to do, says in verse 7: "Thou shalt not tempt the Lord thy God." Jesus knew this ploy of Satan. Sometimes, we just want to jump, right? Sometimes, we just want to give in when life becomes too frustrating for us, and we cannot find another way out.

Years ago, I rented a tiny mountain cottage on Blood Mountain in North Georgia. It was snowing outside one night, so I decided to go out on the back deck and watch it around 10 p.m. When I started to re-enter the back door, I realized that it had locked on me! Here I was, in my pajamas and freezing, and I could not get back inside to the warmth of my fire. Furthermore, I was a long distance away from the nearest cabin, so even if I screamed to the top of my voice, no one would hear me. The only alternative I had was to jump off the deck and risk breaking a leg, an arm, or any other body part for the drop was about 20 feet down! If I tried to spend the night on the deck until morning (which was a long time off), I would freeze to death! What would you have done? Thankfully, I grew up jumping off the roof of our home and doing the tuck-and-roll maneuver my daddy had taught me from his military days.

So, I jumped! I made it, but then had to walk up to the Lodge and wake the folks up and tell them my story. Embarrassed, I stood there in my pajamas at their front door and told them what had happened. Furthermore, the front door to my cabin was locked and I could not get back in. The manager had to come down and take the lock off the front door to let me in. He said he would replace the door lock the first thing the next morning. I really felt like a heel at that point, but I survived the jump, and I would live to talk about it the next day. The manager was a real sport about it and did not charge me for the trouble.

In Jesus' situation, he knew the mind of Satan and that he was tempting him to do something for show. How many times are we tempted to do similar things? Do we give in to the demands of others, or do we approach life cautiously and courageously from a biblical point of view?

Thirdly, there is the worldly temptation of Satan. Satan takes Jesus up on a high mountain and shows him all the kingdoms of the world. He basically says, "All this could be yours if you will only bow down and worship me." Again, Jesus sees through the temptation and knows that the Father (God) already owns everything, so what is there to gain?

In verse 10 we read, "Then saith Jesus unto him, Get thee hence, Satan: for it is written, Thou shalt worship the Lord thy God, and him only shalt thou serve." At that exhortation, Satan flees from the presence of the Lord and the "angels came and ministered unto Jesus" (verse 11). We must be strong to overcome the wiles of Satan and his angels. How do we do that? By faithfully following the Word of God and living a life in total submission to Him.

I grew up hearing the story of the Tortoise and the Hare. It was one of Aesop's Fables. It tells us that a Hare crossed paths one day with a slow moving Tortoise and challenged him to a race. The Tortoise agreed to race the Hare and so off they went! Of course, through trickery, he Hare was far ahead of the Tortoise so he decided to take a nap, knowing the Tortoise would never catch up to him. Long story short - the Tortoise won the race by endurance and a slow determined movement. I guess the Hare learned a lesson, as did Satan, that you never underestimate the power of one's endurance and ability. Jesus was the Son of God and Satan knew that, but he was willing to take a chance on getting Jesus to change course. Jesus never wavered from the teachings of God. The Hare's over-confidence teaches us a lot if we would only listen. Stay the course and Christ will see you through, no matter what you may endure this day.

God bless you on your journey today.

Epitaph

This passage of scripture from Hebrews 11:4 is to be placed on my grave marker after my departure.

> *"By faith...he obtained witness that he was a righteous man, God testifying of his gifts; and by it he being dead yet speaketh."*

May this be my testimony to the life God has allowed me to live here on earth for Him. I give to Him all my praise and adoration.

Charles E. Cravey, March 2024

ABOUT THE AUTHOR

The Rev. Dr. Charles E. Cravey holds the Ph.D. from Trinity Theological Seminary, the M.S.L. (Master of Sacred Literature) from Trinity, a B.S. degree in Sociology from Georgia Southern University (Statesboro, Georgia), and the A.A. degree from Abraham Baldwin Agricultural College in Tifton, Georgia.

Dr. Cravey has now completed his eighteenth book with this offering and has already started work on #19! Writing is his passion. Weaving the story of our lives into poetry, short stories, or essays, gives him the opportunity of expression.

He is also a songwriter/singer/publisher/recording artist/father and husband. He is the pastor of Rosemary Baptist Church in Millen, Georgia, and has been the church's interim for the past ten years, following a 40 year career in the South Georgia Conference of the United Methodist Church as an ordained minister.

His life is Christ and serving Him. To God be the glory!

OTHER PUBLICATIONS BY THE AUTHOR

Kindle Vella book: *Daily Talks for Daily Walks by Dr. Charles E. Cravey* (Online)

The Poet's Pen magazine

The Society of American Poets

The Georgia Poetry Society

Through the Eye of a Needle (Brentwood Press)

Paradigms and Parables (Amazon.com)

Skid Marks (a novel) - Amazon.com

Lessons Learned in the School of Hard Knocks (Amazon.com)

Under the Canopy (Amazon.com)

Pot Liquor Hill and Other Stories

Fruits From the Vineyard (various Georgia newspapers)

Signposts and Disciplines

Living Straight in a Curve Ball World

The Road Less Traveled (Amazon.com)

Diamonds in the Rough

Poems from a Parish Preacher

Keeping the Sabbath

A Voice in the Darkness

Poems, Prayers, and Promises

Memories, Reflections and Words of Hope

Dr. Cravey also has 17 albums of original recorded music to his credit.

www.ingramcontent.com/pod-product-compliance
Lightning Source LLC
Chambersburg PA
CBHW030138170426
43199CB00008B/111